What I've Learned from Your Kids

By Doc Dossman

And What You As Parents Need To Know

Foreword by Gayle Jackson
Mother of NFL Star DeSean Jackson, Philadelphia Eagles

With contributions by Coach Don Norford of
Long Beach Polytechnic High School

Editing Credits: Stacey Jackson-Wade, Lisa Sovory, M.D.,
& Rashida N. Dossman, PA-C

Cover Photography: Stephanie Samiah Taylor

What I've Learned from Your Kids
Copyright © 2010 by Craig A. Dossman, Jr. All rights reserved.
Printed in the United States of America. No part of this book may be used or reproduced in any manner whatsoever without written permission except in the case of brief quotations embodied in critical articles or reviews. For information, visit www.thehardestpilltoswallow.com

ISBN 978-0-9844824-3-6

First Edition: June 2010

LETTER TO MY YOUNG PEOPLE
(you know who you are)

I know many of you are very proud of this book and what it represents. I am just as proud to be the one to speak on your behalf. The ironic thing is, most of you are not going to read this book all the way through. You will probably look through the pictures or text, find your contribution, smile, and then pass the book to your parental unit. That's fine with me. I didn't write this book for you to read anyway. :) I wrote this letter and placed it at the beginning of the book, hoping that if you read nothing else, you will read this advice from me to you.

There are many things that I could say. Many of you are going through many different things, so I'd rather not choose a particular group. I was inspired by a friend by the name of Mr. Andrew Cohn. He gave me something to think about. It is a piece of advice that can help each and every one of you. It is something that you can carry with you for the rest of your life.

Many of you are making very important decisions in your life. Many of you are making poor choices. Some of these choices are being made in the moment with no rhyme or reason. If I asked you why, I'd get the *Kanye West Shrug. Remember when he gave Taylor Swift back the microphone? Yeah, that's you. Some of these decisions involve your sexuality, experimenting with drugs or alcohol, or going to college. Some of you are considering cheating on a test. Some of you are even giving thought to taking your own life.

No matter which life choice is in front of you, remember that your decision today will affect you tomorrow. Tomorrow might be ten years down the line but IT WILL AFFECT YOU. It will affect others as well.

So let me get to my point. I want you to consider something for me. Think about what is most important to you. As a matter of fact, I want you to get a pen and paper. I'll wait. Seriously: go get a pen and paper! I really don't ask you guys to do much, so just do it. Pull out a pen and paper.

Write down the ten most important things to you in your life right now. I don't care what they are. Write them down. It might be something that seems simple or stupid. It doesn't matter, just write them down. If it is important to you to make sure that you have every Drake mix-tape that comes out, write it down. If it is important to match your iPhone cover to your outfit each day, then write it down.

Maybe you feel the need to have a G-Shock watch in every single color. Well . . . write it down.

When you finish this list, I challenge you to think about your life ten years from now (as an adult). Fast forward in your mind and now read your list again. How many of these items will still be as important to you ten years from now? This is how you can tell the difference between what's really important and what's just temporary stuff that has you buggin'. Now I want you to cross out those things that won't make the cut in the future. Scribble 'em out completely. Make it so that you can't even read them anymore. The stuff that remains on the list is truly more important. This stuff can be considered when making life decisions. I'm not here to judge you or to tell you what should be important or what should make that list. I am simply offering a guideline you can follow to stay true to yourself and to remind you what is really important (no matter what it is).

Fold this piece of paper up and keep this edited list with you at all times. The next time your are faced with an important decision, pull it out, read it again, and then think about how the decision you are about to make will affect these high priority items. How will this affect _____ (*plug in the most important item here*). If you consider what is truly important when you decide, you put yourself far ahead of the game. You put yourself in a separate league from your peers. You will eliminate unnecessary stress. You will realize what isn't worth crying over. Maybe what that person thinks about you really doesn't matter. HIGH KEY!!! Maybe the kids that pick on you and give you such a hard time don't really matter in the big picture.

I love you. I am on your side. I want you to be happy with yourselves and to stand firmly behind the choices you make. Before you hand this book over to your parent, read the chapter called "Off-Limits For Parents". I wrote this chapter especially for you. This letter is a setup to trick you into reading that chapter. Yeah Son, I got you. I think you will find this chapter MAX helpful. If you guys really like it, I may start my next book as a continuation of that chapter. It'll be just for you!

God bless,

Doc Dossman

P.S. At your next appointment, or if I see you in the street, I'm going to ask to see your list! Don't let me catch you without it!

TABLE OF CONTENTS

ACKNOWLEDGEMENTS	3
FOREWORD	7
PREFACE	11
NEGLECT	19
SEXUALITY AND MOLESTATION	29
DON'T BE SO IGNORANT... PLEASE!!!	53
ASSUMED FAMILIARITY	59
WHERE ARE THE FATHERS	69
COPING WITH PRESSURE	85
KIDS WITH SWAGG	99
OFF-LIMITS FOR PARENTS	125
SPORTS & CHARACTER DEVELOPMENT	135
RED OR BLUE PILL	145
SLANG DICTIONARY	157
AFTERWORD	169
"SHOUT OUT" SCRAPBOOK	183
TESTIMONIALS	201
ABOUT THE AUTHOR	245

ACKNOWLEDGEMENTS
"This book would have been impossible without you."

My sweet wife Rashida was so patient with my late nights, and I want to thank her for her support in writing this book. Thank you for keeping things quiet for me so that I could write. Your critical eye really came in handy for me on this project. Your editing was crucial during the home stretch. I really appreciate you and your perspective!

To my wonderful parents, Dr. & Mrs. Craig A. Dossman, Sr. You are my original instructors. Before I met all of these young people and their parents, you were there.

I want to thank Coach Don Norford for his words of encouragement, prayers and support over the years. You are my mentor and my friend. You confirmed for me that this project was God-inspired.

Much love to Rob Shock. You were there with me from the very conception of the idea to write. We were going to do this together but I understand. Your friendship and support for me over the years has been overwhelming. I am humbled to have a friend like you. You are my brother.

To Jasmine Johnson and True Seven Creative: you have helped educate me and sacrificed many hours of your time because you believed in me and what this project represents. Thank you.

What I've Learned from Your Kids

To my supportive friends: Mia Doeve, Alice Green, and my unsung heroes. You gave invaluable feedback and advice on this project. I appreciate your honesty during this process.

To my staff at Alternative Healthcare Solutions: Dr. Damon Anthony, Georgina Montufar, Linda Hebert, Tramaine Lee, and Teri Noeum. Thank you for covering for me, so that I could make my deadlines or conduct interviews. I could not have made the time for this unless you helped me with my full plate.

To my contributors: Stacie Duchene-Alexander, Shani Jackson, Chris Barboza, and Crystal Irving. Your contribution to this project is priceless. Your credentials only enhance my credibility. For this I am grateful.

Thanks to Amina Smith and *The Big Homey*, Dontae Ealy, for all your help with the Slang Dictionary! Niiiiiice!!! To all my young people, who shall remain nameless, you know who you are, I could not have done this without you. You did this because you thought it might help someone else. For this I am not only thankful, but also proud of you.

I want to thank Gayle Jackson for writing such a beautiful foreword for this book. I am flattered that you think so highly of me.

Thanks to Samiah Photography for your patience. I know working with such a large group was challenging. The kids loved you!

Acknowledgments

Thanks to Kirby Lee and Image of Sport for always giving me nice pictures of all my kids. You are brilliant at what you do.

If you asked to remain anonymous, I still want to thank you. You know who you are and how you contributed. Thank you!

To Dr. Lisa Sovory: I cannot thank you enough. I don't know how you did it. You are a devoted wife to your husband. You are an amazing mother to your children. You are a freakin' specialist in Neurology, yet you somehow found time to sacrifice!!! You took this project on as if it were your very own to make sure that I put my best foot forward. You are a true friend, and I am truly grateful for what you have contributed to this project.

Last but not least, to my editor, Stacey Jackson-Forde. I am so grateful for what you have done for this project. I thought I was proud of my book before we met! Now I am proud of this book. I have learned so much about writing and even myself, because of you. Thank you so much! I look forward to working with you again. With so many meeting hours invested, I am also happy to say that I have made a new friend.

FOREWORD

Imagine the sense of security in knowing there is a highly trained and experienced doctor waiting for your call in case of an emergency. It would be reassuring to know, that – just like in the good old days – the doctor would bring the medicine to your home, or that perhaps you could find the cure on your tabletop or in your backpack, or written about in the bookshop. Quite frankly, this book is the cure for what hinders open communication between parent and child.

In this case, the doctor providing the medicine is Dr. Craig A. Dossman, affectionately known, loved and respected as "Doc". His latest labor of love entitled "What I've Learned From Your Kids" is the most up-to-date guide on how our children think and what they really feel. Outside the initial investment of this book, the doctor's advice is free and there is no bill for his services. The fact is: he loves YOU and more importantly YOUR CHILD. This is why he decided to write this prescription for us and why we chose to read it.

I had the pleasure of meeting Dr. Dossman at one of the many Long Beach Polytechnic High School football games. He is there, working diligently, side-by-side with student athletes. He treats, teaches and prepares our kids physically and challenges them mentally so they can compete at the highest levels of high-school sports: the state, national and world competitions. Week after week, he dedicates his knowledge, time, money and efforts. He is ready, willing and able to be that positive, healthy and wholesome male role model our kids so desperately need.

What I've Learned from Your Kids

My son, DeSean Jackson, graduated from Long Beach Poly High School in 2005 and excelled in baseball and football. Fortunately, he benefited from Dr. Dossman's sports medicine services. He earned a full athletic scholarship to the University of California at Berkeley in 2005 and was drafted by the Philadelphia Eagles in 2008. He started as a rookie, garnered national attention and set a new Eagles rookie record in receiving yards. To this day, Dr. Dossman is his personal doctor, mentor and friend. If you are around him for any length of time, it is evident how much our children love and deeply care about him. He is their mentor. We are blessed and highly favored to be in his company.

In this book, the doctor openly shares with you – the reader – his conclusions, recommendations and solutions on why the generation gap is so deep and wide between parent and child, and how to bridge that gap.

If we take the time to read and learn from what he has poured out of his heart, we can start opening the lines of communication with our own kids. These precious words can help us today and urgently change the world for our children tomorrow.

This book teaches:

- the do's and don'ts of how to reach your children right where they are
- how to get your children to talk about their intimate thoughts and tell you what they really feel
- how to reevaluate your relationship with your children

Foreword

- how to make a better relationship with your children, grandchildren or other family members

It is a must-read guide for all parents. No matter where you are on the "open communication scale" of one to ten, you can learn techniques from this book.

Whether you personally know Doc or not, I believe you will appreciate his formula for YOUR child's immediate success. He has obviously been there when we were too busy to unravel the innermost thoughts of our children's minds. As he explains in this dose of conversations, our children are crying out through their actions and deeds. They need more love, time, and attention – and so do we. We can all use a personal doctor on our team and, ladies and gentlemen, this one is for YOU.

Thank you very much, Dr. Dossman. Thanks for caring and sharing your love with the world.

- Gayle Jackson, Mother of NFL Star DeSean Jackson

PREFACE

This book is vital for anyone wanting to "reach out" to a young person. Parents, teachers and pastors - established authority figures in the life of a young adult - are my target audience.

This book is my gift to you. I have learned so much from you and your kids over the years. I only want to give back what you have unknowingly taught me. I am not a certified child expert. I am not a psychologist. I have not conducted any peer-reviewed scientific research. Factual statements will be cited and professional opinions will be referenced for further consideration.

The premise of this book is based on my personal experience with your children. I am sharing and giving back what I've learned from them and not from some book or research study. This is why I have titled this book "What I've Learned from Your Kids." I am sharing my personal research via my affiliation with the nationally recognized athletic program at Long Beach Polytechnic High School and other local schools in Southern California. The contributors of this book - childcare providers, educators, coaches, parents, your children, and me - ARE THE REFERENCES.

IF YOU THINK YOU DON'T NEED TO READ THIS BOOK BECAUSE YOU HAVE IT ALL TOGETHER, YOU SHOULD DEFINITELY READ THIS BOOK. IN FACT, YOU SHOULD READ THIS BOOK THREE TIMES. I WROTE IT SPECIFICALLY FOR YOU.

Who am I? Why do I have such strong opinion and conviction? They call me Doc. I am a specialist in Sports Medicine, currently practicing my art and applying my skill in the heart of Long Beach, California. Most of my patients, roughly 70%, are athletes competing at all different levels: Pop Warner, high school, college, professional, world class, and Olympic. The majority of these athletes range from 12 to 28 years of age. In general, my patients are your kids. I deal with your kids all day, every day. I interact with them when they are injured and vulnerable. I am often responsible for being more than just their doctor. To some, I am a friend, to others, a father figure, a confidant, a chaplain or a big brother. I simply make myself available to fill the missing spaces and offer treatment for their needs.

Sometimes, they cry in the treatment room. We pray together in the treatment room too. They open up to me in the treatment room. At times, I am their unofficial therapist. These interactions have taught me about how they cope with adversity, injury, and internal and external pressure. Your kids are each an encyclopedia (a Wikipedia) of information about themselves. We can learn so much from them. Admittedly, I am not a child psychologist or a formal child-development specialist. I am your kid's "Doc" and I love each one of them. I listen and learn. I think God has blessed me to be in this position so that I will be well equipped when my children are of age.

What makes this book so different? How will this information differ from so many other parenting books that you could pick up? I am so glad that you asked! Most research studies are not based on a wide variety or spectrum of ethnicities.

Preface

Kids from diverse socioeconomic backgrounds are rarely represented in these studies. This is because in many communities, going to "therapy" or "the shrink" is considered TABOO. If you need therapy, something is wrong with you. You need to be *crazy* to see the therapist! This is a prevalent and widely accepted ideology in many cultures.

Access to health insurance is also an issue with a huge disparity in coverage for many people, especially in the United States. If there is minimal to zero health insurance coverage in a household, it is highly unlikely that there are adequate finances to pay for therapy sessions. As a result, the kids sampled in most psychological studies represent a small piece of the puzzle. There is a large void of representation of "the others" (inner city youth, minorities, middle to lower class, etc.). The information shared in this book is meant to fill this void.

In my practice, I treat the kids that actually represent the majority, and not a small privileged section of the population. The kids in my sports practice represent "the others". What isn't discussed in therapy is oftentimes brought up in the next safest environment. My treatment room is one of those alternatives. When a kid comes to my office, they are usually injured and distressed. If they want to get back in the game, they must learn to trust me. Because I am on their side and here to help them, they also learn to like me. Because of their injuries, they are anxious and under pressure. Coping mechanisms are not yet fully established in that of a child, so these kids are quite vulnerable in my office. I see a side of them that you do not see.

The trust of a vulnerable kid is a powerful privilege that I do not take lightly. They have a safe place in my office to open up. They trust me and they also understand doctor-patient confidentiality. I get the *real* scoop directly from the source. Because these kids don't go to formal therapy, it is the teachers and coaches that usually shoulder the weight of monitoring the mental and spiritual health of this generation. I think you should be very careful when you disregard the advice or concerns of your child's teacher or coach. They can be very helpful in gaining information that might just save your child's life.

When it comes to parenting and having a relationship with your child, he or she teaches me what works, as well as what does NOT work. Over the past decade, I have learned many valuable lessons working with the kids in my industry. Some lessons I've learned from the children, while others I've learned directly from dealing with you: the parents. When I come across an outstanding child, most of the time, I interview his or her parents. For both professional and personal reasons, I have asked for tips to duplicate the same results. With the help of these parents, I am growing into an excellent father. I have learned more from them than they will ever know. Sharing this information is the least I can do. I pray you will read it with an open mind.

Throughout this book, you will find insight from professionals of various industries that deal directly with young people. You will read input from a social worker, a probation officer, a high school teacher, and a coach. I will introduce you to Coach Don Norford. He is a friend who, over the years, has become a mentor. He is the one who encouraged me to pen

Preface

this book and offered his full support. I have learned so much from Coach Don, and I give credit to his wisdom for much of my success in reaching the kids that come into my office. We have worked together since 2003. I worked with his running backs in football. I have also been the team doctor for his track and field teams at Long Beach Poly High School in Long Beach, CA.

Coach Don is the first assistant coach to receive the National Football League (NFL) award for High School Coach of the Year. Thirty years later, he continues to inspire and motivate kids. He is credited with sending more than 50 of the kids he has coached to the NFL. These NFL athletes include an impressive list of renowned football players:

<p align="center">Will McGinest, Cleveland Browns
DeSean Jackson, <i>Philadelphia Eagles</i>
Winston Justice, <i>Philadelphia Eagles</i>
Pago Togofau, <i>Philadelphia Eagles</i>
Marcedes Lewis, <i>Jacksonville Jaguars</i>
Omar Stoutmire, <i>Washington Redskins</i>
Samie Parker, <i>Kansas City Chiefs</i>
Manuel Wright, <i>New York Giants</i>
Donovan Warren, <i>New York Jets</i>
Terrence Austin, <i>Washington Redskins</i>
Jason Bell, <i>New York Giants</i>
Marques Anderson, <i>Oakland Raiders</i></p>

Coach Don is a respected pillar of the Long Beach community; he has spent the past 67 years there. He is the most unassuming and humble man that I know. If you'd seen him on the street, you would never guess that his track record is filled with accolades. As a sports practitioner and a mentor, I would be proud to be just like him. Don is my top "go-to guy" when I hit a wall with the kids. Everyone should have someone like Coach Don in his or her life.

I completed an extensive interview with Coach Don for his input and expert advice on the topics covered in this book. He has taught me many things and much of what he says adds further validity to my points.

"This is your last chance. After this, there is no turning back. You take the blue pill . . . the story ends. You wake up in your bed and believe whatever you want to believe. You take the red pill . . . you stay in wonderland and I show you how deep the rabbit hole goes. Remember, all I'm offering is the truth. Nothing more."

- Morpheus, *The Matrix*

NEGLECT

I looked at her in the eyes and asked, "You are very lonely aren't you?" As tears rolled down her face again, she looked away and said, "YES."

This is a touchy subject, but I seem to find a way to make everything touchy. Nobody wants to hear this one. Nobody wants to be guilty of it. Neglect. In this case, I define neglect as "not paying proper attention to someone, or disregarding them." I hear of this quite a bit, and there is one common denominator that appears in cases of neglect more than any other: the teenage mom. I am not talking about teenage mothers per se. Rather, I am speaking of the mother who had their child at an early age, but may not necessarily be young anymore. If you are the mother I am thinking of, more than likely, you are NOT married. You might be about 32 to 37 years old and your child might be about 14 or 15 years old. You probably gave up quite a bit of your childhood and some freedoms when you decided to "keep the baby." Maybe, because of your religious background or culture, you had no choice. Well, nonetheless, you missed out on some things (ball games, prom, clubbing) and that itch is still there, because it hasn't been scratched. The things that are beginning to get old to all of your peers are still desirable to you. You've been missing out. As soon as your kids are seemingly old enough to babysit themselves, you are "Free at last! Free at last! Thank God almighty, free at last!"

You can be found at parties, clubs, concerts, and weekend ski trips with your friends; everywhere else that your child is

NOT. You gettin' it poppin' baby! I think it's okay for me to still use that word. Maybe not. You are free and relieved and, somehow, you feel deserving. You feel that it's your time. You also feel that you should do it for yourself; after all, you've been dedicating yourself to the kid since you were a kid. Am I talking to you? I actually have a close personal friend who fits this description perfectly, but I cannot tell her anything. She just doesn't want to hear it. She somehow thinks that as long as she fulfills all her mandatory motherly duties, she is free to fly. As long as she makes dinner available, transports the children to practice or picks them up from school, then anytime away from that is off the clock.

When she is off the clock, she leads a fairly active nightlife. She has been involved in various relationships and finds a way to justify keeping them a secret from her two daughters. It's usually the same line many single moms use. "I try not to have a bunch of different men coming in and out my house. I don't want to send the wrong message, or for the children to get attached to someone I might not see myself with long term."

Oh, how kind of you! So thoughtful. So considerate. I'm sorry but you must be smoking crack cocaine if you believe this is true. If you deal with a bunch of different men, you have some issues. If you deal with the type of men that you cannot bring home to meet your daughters, you have some issues. If you continue (at your age) to deal with men that you might not see yourself with for the long term, you have some issues.

Neglect

I gave my friend all of these things to consider. Somehow she feels that she isn't ready to take the next step with the guy she's been dating for over a year. She admitted to being noncommittal. Herein lies the problem: two young ladies that have no male example at home. They don't really know what they should look for in a man/boyfriend. They haven't exactly been able to learn by mom's example, because she's too busy being sneaky. The funny thing is that they know. These kids are so observant. You can feed them all the lines you want, but they see right through you. When you find this out, it will break your heart, but right now it is their hearts that are breaking because you are too busy running the streets and sneaking around, "Catching up for lost time." So here is a perfect opportunity to lead by example and you are blowing it.

If you let your kids meet whom you have chosen as your person of interest, they can learn what to look for in a mate. They can watch and learn what is to be tolerated and what is not. They can learn who doesn't even deserve the time of day. If they don't learn these things, you are asking for trouble. Their choices will be based upon what arouses them sexually and who looks most attractive. They will be simply looking for company to fill the void that you have left.

I recently spent some one-on-one time with my friend's daughter. We discussed things related to her and her life. We talked about my book and the research I was doing. I read a few things to her, and she instantly identified with so much that all her barriers came down. I had a foundation of familiarity, previously established, and we connected. She began to answer some of my survey questions. After a while, things got more personal and the questions became more specific. I was able to ask about specific issues that her mother had been confiding in me about - that the daughter was having trouble at school and was said to have a poor attitude. She was also accused of "shutting everyone out" at home.

There was not much denial going on during this chat. The daughter was, in fact, having issues both at home and at school. Her home issues prevented her from being able to lean on her mom for support to remedy the academic issues. Everyone just pointed the finger at her as being the one who had issues or blamed it on going through puberty. Was it hormonal? Maybe. Nobody took the time to do their homework and even if they had, maybe it wouldn't have mattered, because she had already shut them out.

It turned out she was being bullied at school. She attends a school for gifted children and there is a different kind of bullying that goes on there. There are no thugs, but in these schools academic bullying takes the place of the bullying we are familiar with. Academic bullying occurs when students chastise the kids that raise their hands to ask questions or for not understanding concepts. If they don't answer correctly when called upon, they are teased and laughed at. Some bullies might say, "That's so easy! How could you not know that? What an idiot!" This is pretty intimidating to a young person amongst their peers.

Neglect

Long story short, she was too intimidated to ask questions and never got the help she needed to succeed in the class. Her mom didn't go to that type of school. How could she know anything about this?

"Why didn't you tell your mother that you were having trouble?" I asked. She told me that she wasn't talking to her mom and didn't want to ask for any help from her. There were a plethora of reasons why she was upset with her mother. Her major complaint was that her mom was never home. With full emotion in her voice, she said, "She is always out. She didn't even come home last night. She never tells me anything. I never know where she is. I have no idea who she is out with or who she is dating."

I was not really blown away by how much she knew. I knew where her mom was going and whom she was dating. What was interesting was that when she asked her mom to stay home, she felt she was being a nag or an annoyance. She said that when her mom stayed home, she acted restless, like she didn't really want to be there. Her mom would say things like, "Okay, I'm here! Are you happy? Well, now what?" This wasn't very welcoming, so the daughter decided never to bother her mother with staying home again. She decided that things were just the way they were going to be. Mom goes out, and daughter stays home to keep an eye on little sister. She even made the comment, "I'm not her mother. I shouldn't have to raise her. It's unfair."

Wow! To hear a child say that was sobering. I dared to take our conversation deeper by asking her what her single most regret was. She paused and then said, "Having sex." She said she had been 14 at the time and did it because she thought he would stay with her - as in, stay around physically - and she was so lonely. She confessed that the guy dumped her the next day. At that point, she began to cry. I asked her what she regretted most about having sex. (Some kids have confessed that sex led to pregnancy and consequently, an abortion that they never go a day without thinking about. Others say they contracted a STD). My little friend said she regretted using sex to fill the void her mother left. If she'd known that the boy was going to later reject her, she would not have given herself to him. She would have simply asked her mom to stay home and endured being rejected by her instead. I looked at her in the eyes and asked, "You are very lonely aren't you?"

As tears rolled down her face again, she looked away and said, "YES."

She was saddened by the topic of discussion, yet intrigued by what she was learning about herself. I told her that I had learned that she was lonely, as well as prideful. She had refused to ask her mother for help when she really needed it, because she didn't like to ask anyone for help. She didn't want to cooperate with the teachers at school because they presumed to understand her problems, and she didn't like that. These two things are a dangerous combination, because pride will only enhance or bring about more loneliness. She didn't want to ask her mother to stay home anymore, and she didn't want to ask for help resolving her

Neglect

problems at school. All of this left her feeling alone. Neglect meets self-inflicted loneliness.

So many kids are lonely. Some have no siblings. Many spend hours alone in the house; the "latchkey kid" is no rare breed. These kids are lonely. They feel neglected. You think you do enough, but you are mistaken. The consequence of this situation is the neglected child becomes resentful. They make decisions based on spite and resentment rather than on logic or anything you have bothered to take the time to teach them.

This topic saddens me. I had an interview scheduled with another kid after I took my friend's daughter home. I was so emotionally drained. I rescheduled the interview and went home to bed. I didn't even have anything in me to write. Writing this chapter felt like repeating myself to my friend all over again. My friend is not much different than some of you. Because of this, I know that it will take much to convince you that you chose to "do your thing" prematurely. I would like to encourage you to wait until your kids have gone away to college. This is all the more reason to encourage them to leave for school. Sure, you've got catching up to do. It's just that right now is NOT the time. You have got some educating to do. You have to keep them company. Show them how to become mature and responsible. They only know what you tell or show them. Everything else is learned in the streets or on television. Most television programs viewed by kids really have nothing good to teach them. They spend hours watching MTV, VH-1 and BET. And if they aren't watching TV, they're on the Internet.

So what should you do now? Make yourself available and when you make yourself physically available, don't become emotionally unavailable. Be there for your child. If you don't, someone else will, at least for the moment. They are making the wrong decisions in your absence. I know it sounds like I'm being extreme, but your 14-year-olds are having sex because they are lonely.

I don't care how impressed you are with your child's level of maturity. My grandmother always said, *"Idle hands are the devil's workshop."*

My friend is actually impressed that her daughters seem to be wise beyond their years. They actually are pretty impressive. But at what cost? These girls are pretty much raising themselves. They wake themselves up for school, do their own laundry (including mom's), wash the dishes and clean the house. I'm sure many of you wish your 14 year olds were on "autopilot" like this. Unfortunately, these kids are being forced to grow up prematurely, because their mother is absent. She is in denial of her absence, because she is doing the bare essentials of her duties.

Some parents tend to feel good about doing "their job," but it's the other stuff that makes you a "mom." Spend time with them. Get to know them. Stay home tonight, even if they act like they don't care. Trust me. They care. If you are dating someone, show your children the type of person they should

Neglect

look for in a mate. Lead by example. They watch you more than they hear you.

If you fit this category, you are not much different than your child. You are lonely and searching for something to fill a void (just like the 14-year-old who lost her virginity). You are lonely when you are not getting what you want or need. You can be lonely in a crowd. You know what it's like to be lonely, so why subject your child to this as well? Go home. I hope you are not on an island beach somewhere reading this while your kids are at home. Go home, now.

COACH DON NORFORD
just be true to your word

A lady coach came up to me at a track meet, and we greeted each other. We started talking and it got around [the team]. Two of the girls boldly came up to me and wanted to talk about their race. I introduced the lady to them and told her I had to get back to my girls. She understood and left.

That was a big thing to the girls. They wanted to see if I was "true to my word" about keeping them first. They wanted to see if I was going to tell them to move on, because I was getting my Mack on. They test you like that. When things happen like that, you use it to your advantage to get closer to those kids.

SEXUALITY & MOLESTATION

The little girl that was penetrated by her uncle at the age of six feels like damaged goods...

I'm really not sure where to begin with this chapter. Things could get pretty explosive. To be honest, many of my interviews have left me stunned and heartbroken. I will admit, that at one time, I actually went into a slight depression. Many of these kids are very close to my heart. I sat on this information for quite some time, because I couldn't bring myself to sit in front of my computer and replay their stories in my head. This isn't a topic pursued in my interaction with young people, but it seems to be the source of so many of their issues that it comes up from time to time. The topic of sexuality can go very deep and be very broad. When covering this area, issues of incest, molestation, rape, promiscuity and homosexuality cannot be ignored.

It might blow your mind if you knew how many kids have had abortions, been treated for sexually transmitted diseases, or even been raped by a close relative (a cousin, one of your siblings, or even your spouse). Some of you have absolutely no idea whether your kid is sexually active or not. Sure, a few of you are bold enough to ask the question, yet how many are getting honest responses? Some would prefer to assume than to know. Some continue to believe that ignorance is bliss.

Many parents are split on opinions about this topic. Some have no problem with young people and sex. Some might even be comfortable with the idea of a kid with an alternative sexual lifestyle. Many homes apply their religious convictions and morals to the topic and form fairly strong opinions. No matter your stance, in today's world, sexuality is an integral part of the life of a young person. We live in an age of information; they have access to so much more than we could even have imagined when we (you) grew up. Most of their initial exposure and sex education comes from pornography. As early as the fifth and sixth grade, kids are on the Internet or watching DVDs. Some are watching porn from your private stash. Maybe I should call it your personal stash. We can't call it private anymore, can we?

Rather than getting into the details about who is doing whom and how, there are better questions to ask that can help you as parents (and as authority figures). The dirty details will get us nowhere but a land of more concern and maybe even some liability issues. The question is what role do you have in the sexual development/maturity of your child? How important is your role, if at all? The most productive way to deal with this is to figure out a way to be of assistance, not to pass judgment.

Over the years, I've learned that there are some obvious patterns and trends when it comes to kids and their sexuality.

1. *They are not learning about sex from you.*

If they are lucky, they can recall sex education from middle school. Sex Ed basically covered the physiology of the reproductive system, as well as information on sexually transmitted diseases. If the class was really progressive, they were even exposed to condoms. If they were taking sex education as early as middle school, would you say that high school is a bit late for the "birds and bees" speech? They have so many questions. Rather than come to their parents, they go to the Internet. Once they get on the Internet, that's it! There is nothing you can say to them. They can learn more about sex than you can teach them. Okay, I'm lying to you. They don't really know the truth about sex. There is way too much information. All they know is that they are very confused and their heads are spinning.

2. *What they learn and digest from the Internet, they discuss with their friends at school.*

"Babies educating babies, on grown-folk stuff." Sex is the topic of so many conversations. However, kids tell me they would never bring up that conversation with you. They say that they can't bring up conversations about anything with you.

"We don't talk much about anything."

"Communication lines? What's that?"

They learn what isn't acceptable from overhearing your conversations and from religious stances taken at church. The extent of your talks with them, if there have been any at all, have been one-way communication. You told them NOT to do it. Maybe you told them it was a sin. Maybe you told them it was for married people and then left it at that.

The best story I've heard about a "sex-talk" was one given while in a McDonald's drive thru. That's about a five-minute speech, maybe? Well, it was pretty productive because the kid learned that there were three types of sex: oral, vaginal, and anal. He also learned that he could make a baby or catch a sexually transmitted disease if he didn't wear a condom. This is actually, by far, the best "birds and the bees talk" I have heard.

Many parents have never even touched the subject. Some have waited until either their kid got pregnant or they caught them having sex. Many parents seem to be more reactive than proactive. That's unfortunate, because their timing is kind of off.

3. *Sadly, many kids have been sexually molested before the age of ten.*

I know a young lady; we will name her "Carla." She is a sweet Mexican young lady. Very kind hearted and loving. You couldn't imagine the things that she has endured. At the age of 6 years old, her teenage uncle began molesting her. This was her father's baby brother. It started when her father left her at her grandmother's house to go spend time with his lady friend. Carla's uncle was always at her grandma's house.

He would babysit her when she spent time there. He began fondling her and touching her in various areas. He would pretend it was a game as he giggled joyously, encouraging her to laugh as well. He was encouraging her to not be afraid "this is fun." Carla really didn't know what or how to feel. She was uncomfortable. Eventually, her uncle laid her down and proceeded to penetrate her vaginally. He told her not to scream and frightened her with threats to kill her father. When he was done, he ordered her to pretend she was asleep, so when her father returned he would have no suspicions. Her tears would have been a cold give away.

> *She felt violated. "I am not a virgin. I'm broken, tainted, dirty, unworthy of love and relationships."*

Carla was fearful of what might happen if she told her father, so instead, she confided in her five-year-old brother. Her baby brother confessed that he had also been fondled by the very same family member! Carla thought she had convinced her brother to keep her secret until she came home one day. When she walked in, her father jumped on her and began to beat her up as never ever before. "I thought he was going to kill me!" Carla said. Her father was furious at her, because she didn't tell him that this was happening. "Did I do something wrong? I thought I was the one being molested!" she cried. She was only seven years old at the time.

She felt violated. "I am not a virgin. I'm broken, tainted, dirty, unworthy of love and relationships." Due to her Mexican culture, there were strong ties to the Catholic Church. Abstinence is strongly encouraged. No words could ever comfort Carla.

When Carla turned 15 years old, her father allowed her uncle to live with them because he was having some problems. She felt so betrayed. "Did my father not remember what this man had done to his precious daughter?" Apparently all was forgiven. She continues to live in fear and is always uncomfortable. She says, "I felt that my father cared more about his little brother than his child." It was this very realization that may have hurt her more than anything else.

Her relationship with her uncle was more than poisonous. She could never forgive. Carla was very disrespectful to him. She always tried to attack him with her words, knowing he was defenseless because of what he had done to her. Her uncle was later murdered. Now things are forever unresolved. Her father went into a deep depression and didn't seem to care about much anymore. The way he handled his brother's death, made his children feel as if they didn't matter. It seemed as if her father cared more about his brother than his children.

She felt alone, neglected, and was left to care for her younger brother. Carla says that as a result of telling her father about the molestations, he became overly protective and strict. He always kept them inside the house. She regrets how much this ruined her social life during high school.

> *"What happened to me happened at home."*

She also feels that her father never comforted her when she needed. This has left a void to fill. She tends to look for other men to fill this void.

Sexuality & Molestation

So many children are finding ways to fill these voids of attention, love, acceptance, comfort, affection, and safety, in places that parents would never approve of. Parents tend to be too busy to disapprove. Many parents want to protect their child from such dangers, but always look to the wrong places. Nobody wants to believe that it could be a stepfather, an uncle, or member of the clergy. Nobody wants to believe that the babysitter or nanny is being inappropriate. These are the people that we have chosen to let close to us. We let them into our safety net.

Some kids don't count this encounter (with most likely a relative) as their first sexual experience. Some, regrettably, do. They feel their innocence was stolen from them. Once it's gone, that is it. Many of them go on to live a promiscuous lifestyle.

Young boys that were molested by another male feel like damaged goods. Many feel, that because of what they have done (or what was done to them), they are now homosexuals. They either go on to live this lifestyle, or they run from themselves by chasing as many "skirts" as they can; hoping that each conquest will give them the manhood they lost years ago.

The little girl that was penetrated by her uncle at the age of six feels like damaged goods. She can go on several paths, as can the boys. She might feel that with her innocence lost, she has nothing to lose, so why not pursue a life of promiscuity if she is already tainted. Some vow they will never be vulnerable to a man again and put themselves in the position of the man. Many of these young girls turn into what you may know as a "dyke." Today they call them "studs." These young ladies take on the very persona and essence of a man. They walk, talk, and dress like a man. By claiming the dominant role in their relationships, they find protection and refuge.

There is extensive psychological damage done to these kids that is never addressed. Some of you know about what happened to your kid, others of you do not know. Most of you have done absolutely nothing to address the kid's psychological issues. Do you know what one of the main issues connected to what happened to them is? Well, at least one issue is resentment towards you. Yes, they feel that you didn't protect them. Most of them were molested while you were out "living your life." You may have dropped them off at a friend or a relative's house so you could go out - many of you are single parents who are still going to clubs, parties and concerts, or going out on dates.

Even at the early age of six, kids feel that you are clearly pawning them off on someone else. Some say their experiences could have been prevented. If you had only spent more time with them, instead of leaving them over at someone else's house. This takes me back to the section where I spoke about neglect. Please revisit if necessary.

Now, there is one other psychological factor that occurs, and it is the most powerful - the number one issue - connected to this negative experience (molestation). Can you guess what it is? It is how the child learns to feel about him or herself.

Sexuality & Molestation

As I write this book, I have been sharing various chapters with people to get their feedback as a form of research. I consulted with parents, teachers, social workers, and more parents! They are really my target audience, so what better barometer than to check the temperature of those to whom this book is written. I did not exactly "consult" but rather evaluate reader responses. The word "consult" seems a little strong because it implies that I'm seeking someone's approval.

One of the evaluated people, whom we will call "Tania," is a part of my control group of readers. I chose her, because she is well connected with young people. She is not a parent. She is a 37-year-old high school teacher in Long Beach, California. Tania knows and truly loves young people. I respect her perspective, so I asked her to read my book.

Tania called me about a week after I emailed her my manuscript. I was anxious to hear her feedback. She seemed distraught and said, "Doc, I need to talk to you about this book." It seemed pretty urgent so I scheduled a lunch with her the next day. I thought that maybe she wanted to set me straight on a few things - the tone in her voice was not encouraging. We met and she started by saying that she enjoyed reading and connecting with my book. She said that it was because of that connection that she felt I could be a good person to talk to. She had been molested and wanted to talk to someone about it. Keep in mind that she is an adult. Tania had been molested at the ages of 8, 11, and 12, all by different men. The story she decided to share was when she was 12 years old. The pastor of her church molested her.

Fast forward to the age of 17: Tania dedicated her life to Jesus Christ and decided to get baptized. Her favorite elder, the one that gave her Bible lessons, agreed to perform the ceremony. She was so excited that he agreed to do this. The day of the baptism, the elder discovered an abscess on his foot that rendered him unable to perform her baptism. She didn't know about the change of plans until she stepped into the water. It turned out that the elder's replacement was her molester, the pastor! She said that the water seemed to boil when she saw him approaching her. She wanted to scream,

"Will my baptism be null and void?"
"Will it count?"
"Will I need to get baptized again?"

I'm not sure I'm qualified to answer those questions. I have my opinions. Tania just wanted to talk. She told me she had kept it to herself for years, until recently. About a month ago, she hosted a rap session at her home with some of her students. (A rap session is a term commonly used for an open discussion forum amongst young people). The rap session started getting heavy with topics of sex and molestation. Tania felt compelled to share her experiences with her kids. She felt a sense of relief for a moment, but then she noticed a few family members in the room: her parents and her big brother had been sitting in the back the entire time!

"What kills me the most is not necessarily reliving those moments. It's the fact that my family has said nothing to me about the rap session! I know [the molestation] was years ago, but shouldn't my big brother and my father have jumped up in a rage to find out who did that to me? Why hasn't my mother inquired anything of me? It's been a month now, Doc! Do they even care?"

After this incident, Tania was more shook up about her father and brother not having concern for her, than about the molestation. She now wonders if they ever really cared. Isn't she their precious little girl? Daddy didn't have anything to say? Doesn't he want to know which one of his friends or colleagues defiled his prize? Doesn't he want to know how many of his friends or colleagues did this to her? NO? This sends a big message to Tania. It confirms her self worth. It tells her how she should feel about herself, even as an adult!

> *. . . the water seemed to boil when she saw him approaching her. She wanted to scream, "Will my baptism be null and void? Will it count? Will I need to get baptized again?"*

After reading my book, she realized that I had heard many stories similar to her own. She felt safe to confess her insecurities to me. She felt so much better after getting this stuff off of her chest. I asked whether she had initiated any discussion about the topic with her family. Tania said she had cornered her mother, who told her, "Let's not go back there." Wow! I asked if she had gotten any counseling or talked to anyone before this. She told me she had talked to her current pastor, but felt her story was too much for him to handle. She didn't really fancy blowing anybody's mind. She said, "He just kept putting his hand on his head and yelling

'WOW!' Occasionally, he would even spin around in his seat. I don't think he can handle it, so I didn't go back."

As I mentioned before, what we do to these kids doesn't always have to affect the way they feel about us. It does however, have a strong impact on how they feel about themselves. *A child with a negative self-image becomes an adult with a negative self-image.* I meet kids like this who have been abused, molested, and neglected. Somehow they still live their lives trying to please you. It is still important for them to get your approval. They still care what you think and take everything you say to heart! I am not kidding you. It is naturally in them to love you and to want you to love them back. No matter what happens. Often, their behavior is 100% about getting your attention. The young ladies I see in abusive relationships, still trying to please their boyfriends, usually have a history of an abusive father from whom they still want approval. It becomes consuming and takes over their lives. Heaven forbid that you should die, and they never get to hear the words, "I love you. You make me so proud!" Think about that.

But Sex is Beautiful . . .

What is really unfortunate is that sex is beautiful. God gave it to us to express our love to our spouse and to procreate (and it feels great too). What is insane is that you will rarely find someone with a positive story about his or her sexual history. Most people have a negative story. I believe that almost all sexual histories are stained with regret. So many people have been the victims of rape or molestation. Most have experienced sex very prematurely and were not prepared to handle the emotional component. Some have regrets because of why they even decided to have sex in the first place. Remember the girl from the NEGLECT chapter? She had sex because she didn't want to be lonely, but that night is now the biggest regret of her life to date. She blames herself because she knows she gave up her virginity for something her mother could have given her (attention). I don't know who has that perfect or ideal sexual history. I do know that, because of their sexual histories, many see sex as overrated and wish they had waited until they were older, or even married. Most of the respect for sex comes a bit late. It comes after the fact, just like some of your attempts at sex talks.

The issue isn't that you haven't bothered to address the topic or are allowing the streets to educate your kid; the issue is that there is a communication problem in the home, period. Nobody is saying anything. Communication is nonexistent. How will we have talks about sensitive subjects like sex when we don't even sit at the table to talk about how the day went? How can you communicate with them when your parents never showed you how? Let's face it, we are all kids trapped in aging bodies. Everyone is a walking experiment. Some experiments went badly, while some just went better than others. The one thing we do know is that nobody TRULY knows what he or she is doing.

It still blows my mind when I think of how many parents seemed so eager to get their hands on this information. The parents who seemed to have the most impressive and balanced kids were just as eager - or even more so - than the parents who are clearly struggling. Some parents just lucked out, and their kids turned out to be less trouble than others. This isn't validation of quality parenthood: sometimes it's just genetics (or luck of the draw). The parents who are in denial and don't feel they need any help, need it the most. I have a chapter just for them: it's about ignorance. Stay tuned . . .

Since every kid is different, no book on child rearing is going to have all the answers. Because I know this, I chose to focus on what all my interviews and stories had in common, rather than on the many juicy details. It is not necessary to parade every sexual indiscretion for your reading pleasure (which could be a book of its own). It is more important for you to see what all the kids have in common: homosexual, heterosexual, male, and female alike:

- They are undereducated and want to know more, but you have not made them feel comfortable enough to initiate the conversation.

- When they do have sex, they can't talk to you about it because they are more concerned about disappointing you than they are about any punishment you might have for them. Some are afraid to tell you about rape or molestation because they don't think you will believe them.

- Many of them are having sex simply to fill a void that you have probably left empty. Either you are too busy and caught up living your own life, or they aren't getting enough attention from you. Maybe you never tell them that you love them. I hear this one quite a bit. That girl who has no daddy in her life will commonly pursue what she is missing in the arms of another man.

- Leaving them at a friend or relative's home is usually when bad stuff happens. Be careful where and when you pawn them off so you can "live your life." They know that they're being pawned off.

Providing a religious upbringing for your kid will foster personal convictions about things like sexual immorality much faster than your preaching or judgment. Introduce them to God so they can have their own personal relationship. Reintroduce yourself to God, so you have a relationship Him and can answer your kid's questions. This is a great foundation builder. Out of all the reasons why kids make the right decisions, the most common factor was because of personal religious and moral conviction. Yes, personal conviction is what allowed them to make the best decision and not your judgmental approach. I know parents that preach hellfire and brimstone to scare their kids out of doing certain things, but making them feel unworthy isn't a good move. You are pushing them away, not only from you but also from God. Be smart. Some parents keep their kids on lock-down and enforce the strictest of rules and regulations. These kids have absolutely no freedom. They usually go wild in college and eventually find a way to do what they want to do.

Most of the kids tell me that their decision to have or not to have sex has absolutely nothing to do with you telling them not to. They are more commonly driven by personal conviction. I am not encouraging you to lift all restrictions and let them do whatever they want to do, but please don't be convinced that the "lockdown" technique is full proof. It certainly is NOT. Most often, they are trying to fill some void in their life, and it is highly possible that it was your job to fill those voids. It is also possible that they aren't even aware they have these voids. It is your responsibility to seek and fulfill; they are still kids. Give them your time. Talk to them. Be honest with them. It is not for me to tell you what to say to them, but I do know that most of you have said nothing.

Please don't be naive. Please don't be ignorant. I can't express this enough. Don't ever assume that you know everything about your kids. Don't ever assume that they are not sexually active. Assumptions lead to trouble. You will always find out when it's too late. Maybe you will find yourself scrambling to find information on teenage pregnancy. Maybe you will find out your kid has already had an abortion with the help of your spouse. Are you the one that won't ever understand? Fortunately, the national teenage-pregnancy rate as well as the abortion rate has plummeted over the last ten years (by at least 36%). This is mainly due to increased education. In the U.S., we have the highest teen pregnancy rate in the world. The CDC (Center of Disease Control) reports that one-third of girls get pregnant before the age of 20.

Teenpregnancy.org, a site managed by the National Campaign to Prevent Teen and Unplanned Pregnancy, states that there are "50,000 teen pregnancies annually. Eight in ten of these pregnancies are unintended and 81 percent are to unmarried teens."

Sexuality & Molestation

It is my opinion, that the least you could do is educate them about contraceptives. If you have said anything to them at all, they probably already know you might disapprove of them having sex. However, you are probably not going to change or lower the chances of them having sex. While you may have no effect on when they have intercourse, you may be able to decrease their chances of teen pregnancy. The numbers and trends on teen pregnancy are quite concerning. When, where, and with whom they have their first sexual encounter is complex. We have already discussed some of the contributing factors. It goes as far as their peers, religious background, family, internet, media, and the individual's personal convictions. Changing the age of their first sexual contact may not be a worthwhile venture, for they may have already had that contact, but at least they are not currently pregnant. This is something that you can help control. Just, please, take an interest. The rest will fall into place (what to do, how to approach this, and where to find information). Don't assume anything, and please take interest.

We could go on and on. We could go in circles all day about rivaling views on this topic. I am only here to tell you what I know, and that is that you (the authority figures) are simply telling them to say, "No," while everyone else (movies, television, internet, and media) are telling them YES, YES, YES!!!! Standing idly by is no way to compete and ignoring the topic isn't a way to protect your kid either.

The BOTTOM LINE is this: they all have regrets about having teenage sex. None of them were prepared to deal with the emotions and feelings that come with the territory.

You should understand this portion of it. You have been there. You have a sexual history. Your history is probably not the path you would suggest for them, and maybe this is why you feel like a hypocrite talking about this with them. You might need to share your personal experiences with them. This will give you credibility, but unfortunately your credibility will come at a small price: your "pure and perfect" image. Oh no! Heavens to Betsy!! Mom/Dad aren't perfect? They're human? I promise this will only make you a bit more approachable, and trust me: you want approachability. This is a time of confusion. There is so much for them to sort through. They aren't just feeling hormonal urges. They also have to deal with outside influences. They may be trying to discover their sexual preference as well. Am I straight, gay, or bisexual? Maybe they are experimenting. The experimental phase doesn't make them gay or bisexual, but it is pretty confusing. Being able to ask questions is key.

FACTS ON TEEN PREGNANCY

- *Teenage mothers are more likely to drop out of high school.*
- *Teenage mothers are more likely to be and remain single parents.*
- *Teenage mothers are more likely to score lower in math and reading into adolescence.*

Sexuality & Molestation

> *Making yourself approachable is paramount if you want a fighting chance to protect them from making the wrong decision.*

Something else that is vital to your kid's sexual balance is that you give them a model of a healthy relationship. This is important for both married and single parents. Kids need to see healthy sexuality modeled. We touched on this briefly in the chapter on neglect. Your self-image and even self-esteem must be at a healthy level to model a healthy sexual relationship. You need to understand what you believe and why exactly you believe it. You need to know exactly what you want your kids to learn about sex/sexuality.

Okay, one more thing. Alcohol. Would you say that alcohol is linked to poor choices? I will keep it short and simple: your kids might be drinking. Do you drink? If yes, then it is even more likely. Many of them get access to liquor from your stash. Protect your stash or get rid of it. I don't mean to downplay the role alcohol plays in sexuality, but we could go all day with this chapter and maybe even write another book.

Let me drive home this point: you have to give and take in a relationship. This means that to have an open and sharing communication with someone, it has to be a two way street. You can't just sponge off all information from them. Like any relationship, most require you to put some of your cards on the table before they are comfortable to put their cards down. You have to become transparent to your kid! You must do this! Becoming transparent is not about coming across as weak or fallible. I know you think this because you feel helpless, or you wonder if maybe you are indeed weak and fallible. The truth is, you are - but that is okay! Don't be in denial of this. Sometimes exposing your weakness can become a strength. Huh? Confusing? Let me explain:

> *If you talk to them about your past mistakes and blunders, they learn a few things. They learn from your mistakes and they also learn that you might actually be able to relate to what they are going through.*

Here is the kicker. If they learn that all the crap they are trying to pull - or plan to - has already been done by you, they will think twice. They need to know that "Mama got game." They need to know that you are not an idiot and that you have been there and done that! These kids think they are onto something new with the games they play. The more you share, the more respect you will develop. It is like building street credibility. Some of you used to sneak out of the house at night. You went to bed and lay underneath the covers FULLY CLOTHED, waiting for your mom to say goodnight. Some of you may have packed your "real clothes" in your backpack and changed in the restroom once you got to school. Others may have sneaked your parent's alcohol to school in a thermos. Some used to leave the house in the car of your friend of the same sex and then met your date, of the opposite sex, around the corner! Trust me, I can go on. When you expose your "old game" to them, you strip them of their weapons. They will learn there are no new games. They will also learn that momma or daddy is the original player.

Sexuality & Molestation

Some say that exposing your old mistakes will give kids permission to mimic them. Maybe they think kids will say:

"Let me make my mistakes, you made yours!"
"Can I have my own path? Can I learn?"
"Can I experience things like you did?"

You know what? You may be right. You might have a valid point, but my mission is to encourage communication, and you are definitely communicating at this point! At least you have a dialogue now. Before, nothing was being said. You think that's a better idea? Maybe fear of confrontation is really the issue causing this lack of or breakdown in communication? Moving on...

Credibility goes a long way with kids. Typically, they think you are stupid and can't relate. I promise that if you create transparency, if they find that you can relate to them, they will come to you. They will talk. They will ask questions so you will not have to ask (the wrong ones). You will no longer be considered clueless. The funny thing is that they will not judge you (like you fear); they will actually look up to you. You have this fear of being judged because you are busy judging them. We do that as humans. We judge people by our own standards or past experiences. We tend to judge based on what we have done and are capable of doing.

I understand that this topic is really overwhelming for you. The content, the reality checks, the fear, the shame, the guilt, the anger, the denial, the disgust, the moral highroad, and the knee-jerk reply: "That's why I told you not to . . ." are all issues that YOU must overcome before you can effectively communicate with an open heart and mind. I am not telling you to come at them like you know everything. Do not communicate to them that you have been there and done that. I am only asking you to create some transparency. Throw your cards out on the table. This will allow them to decide for themselves whether you can relate or not. Please don't bully them into believing that you know. Don't assume you can relate. This is insulting and only belittles their situation. You never want to do this to a young person.

Maybe you have in fact done everything that they have done and are planning to do. The problem is that you don't know the specifics. You must understand going into a conversation that you do NOT understand what your teen is going through right now. You may have lost your virginity at an early age, but you don't know that she is planning to have sex tomorrow night. You do NOT have all the answers. You do NOT have a clue about what your kid is doing, has done, has seen, has experienced, or is planning, until they open up and share. You need to have a strong grip on this reality. You can't help them until they feel comfortable enough to share. While it is true that you may have done some of the same things and be able to relate, until they open up and share, you know nothing. Come with an open mind and zero assumptions. Your child will better respect you and be more willing to share. Parents, you must be prepared to receive and handle the truth.

On another note, I want to share some more interesting information with you. Over the years I've discovered that most young ladies have become sexually active by the time they finish high school. The few that continue to remain abstinent have done so for the following reasons:

- *Fear* of the pain. They have learned this from their friends that have done it.
- Personal religious *conviction*.
- They like the way that guys treat them. They feel like they get more *respect* than the girls that are having sex.

I bring up this point because of the third reason. I found it interesting to hear this. They liked the way they were treated by the boys who know they are virgins. This stands out to me because I have heard quite a few young men say, they pursue the girls who are putting themselves out there. The "fast girls" are known to send out all the signals to initiate contact and, according to the young men, these girls are just as "hungry" as they are. They mention that they don't tend to pursue or even want to bother with the virgins - either out of respect or because some would rather not deal with the emotional hassle.

I mention this because I want you to see the main reason they DO NOT have sex is NOT because you do not want them to. I also want to point out that being a virgin is not as frowned upon in a day and age where sex is encouraged and available to all interested parties. Now that everyone is doing it, the ones that are not are the "different" ones.

Maybe they are envied, because most regret giving away their virginity and wish they had made a different decision.

DON'T BE SO IGNORANT... PLEASE!!!

If you think children are stupid because they don't listen to you, maybe you overestimate yourself...

One of the most interesting scenarios that I encounter is the "clueless parent." These parents are both pathetic and amusing. They are pathetic because their ignorance is frequently voluntary. This refers to parents who would rather be in the dark than "in the know" about what is going on with their child. No parent is really this naive. Maybe they are a bit self absorbed, but not naive. If I'm talking about you, just remember, you were once a teenager. It is amusing to your kid that he or she is getting away with murder right under your nose.

The three most common scenarios I see are the alcoholic, the homosexual, and the sexually promiscuous young girl. These three demographics are all crying out in their own way. They actually want to be noticed. They want to know that you care. They'd love to hear that you are concerned about them. This is the truth. Many of these kids think that you don't care. Some of you think that you are being the "cool" mom or dad, and maybe even want to be your child's friend. You are mistaken. Your child wants parents.

Parents with the attitude that their children are perfect (while others know the truth) are really naïve. Their kids are usually the ones who get in the most trouble. I often ask these kids whether they would tell their parents about their bad habits. Most of the kids feel their parents are more concerned with how the bad habits will make their family look rather than the effects the habits may have on their young bodies and minds.

The kids think, "I already know what Mom/Dad will say." Why should they bother hearing your response?

One thing I have learned is that children are much smarter than we assume. I cannot stress this enough: they are WAY smarter than you give them credit for being. You underestimate them. Your parents underestimated you. We live in an age of information. We have loads of information at the tip of our fingers. We have the Internet and Google on our cell phones, not to mention desktop computers, pocket computers, text messaging, video conferencing, and a bazillion other methods of communication and information distribution. There is much more instant knowledge and information available than when you were their age. You had the card catalog. You had the Dewey decimal system. In the same amount of time that it took you to decide to go to the library, they could have already "googled" the topic and learned more information than they needed.

> *"If you think children are stupid because they don't listen to you, maybe you overestimate yourself."*
> **- Doc Dossman**

I recall a patient who spoke about how her daughter had changed. She said, "My kid used to think I walked on water! There was no wrong I could do! Now she's fifteen and I'm the stupid mother! What's up with that, Doc?" I held my tongue because I could see that she was truly bothered, maybe even hurting. She is not the only one who has admitted this concern to me. I am sure many of you can relate. All that I can say is, you don't walk on water! You never did! So, it's okay for them to grow older and even smarter when they see you for who you really are (possibly, a clueless parent). Like any other type of relationship, after some time, the honeymoon stage is over and the truth is exposed. This is when you learn more about an individual and confirm that nobody is perfect. You make a decision to overlook the negative issues because you have grown to appreciate the positive ones. It's no different when your child turns 15 or 16. They know you. You are all they do know. They have been studying you for 15 years. You underestimate them and you overestimate yourself. Be careful.

Some of you are officers in the church. Some are individuals of high status in your communities, such as politicians, lawyers, doctors, celebrities, and school administrators. You care about your children, but you are quick to protect your reputation. Your kids already know this. Parents of high social status are often, simply too busy to keep up or be concerned with everything their children are doing. If you are always working, or on the road, you may not have given your kids time to share with you. Please, show some interest. Ask questions. Ask the questions that hurt. Ask the questions you are afraid to ask. "Are you gay?" "Do you drink?" "Are you having sex?" Your lack of inquiry comes across as a lack of interest or indifference.

Sometimes you have to do the unpopular thing. I am talking about invasion of privacy; checking their backpack, going through their drawers, or checking their text messages. I'm telling you that it will not be easy, but you could be saving their lives. You might find drugs, condoms, guns, and/or knives. It would blow your mind how many kids feel the need to carry some form of protection. Don't you want to know if your children are afraid for their lives? Don't you want to know if he or she is endangering the lives of others? Do you know whether they are sexually active? Maybe they are using or selling drugs. It is your duty to know these things.

I know that many will have something to say about my lack of respect for privacy. I don't lack respect; I display interest. As your children see it, you lack interest, and this has you in a bind. If you had an open relationship with your children, you would be able to have open discussion with them. If they could come to you about anything, there would be no need for you to take drastic measures, such as prying. I don't generally encourage such blatant disregard for the privacy of another human being, but you need to do what you have to do. Sometimes the end justifies the means.

Some kids don't know how to bring certain topics up in conversation. Many have yet to fully develop their communicative abilities. They simply wait for the topic to come up or be initiated by you. If you don't ask, they may not tell you directly. However, they will certainly tell me and maybe even others. When everyone else seemingly knows everything about your child that you don't, you look bad. Isn't this what many of you set out to avoid in the first place?

Your child needs to know that they can come and talk to you safely. They need to know that you love them, no matter what they say or do. They need to believe that you will only offer assistance rather than judge them or put them down.

Otherwise, they are left with only their own immature assumptions. They need to KNOW. Simply telling them after reading this book is not enough. They need to know it, not just hear it.

You can start by showing them that you are not perfect and that you have and continue to make mistakes. Put some cards on the table. It will build more familiarity and make them more comfortable with you. Another option is to prove it with the little things. If they mess up on something small like forgetting to take out the trash, don't go crazy! When they make mistakes, be careful how you choose to respond. If you lose your cool on the little stuff, why would they come to you about sex or drug experimentation? How can your son tell you that he is curious about other boys? You can't even handle it when they missed curfew by ten minutes. Show them that you can be forgiving, understanding, and love unconditionally. You have to start with the small stuff first.

CRYSTAL IRVING
Director, Long Beach Polytechnic High School Girl's Athletic Program

When a kid is at school for eight hours, we recognize changes quicker than the parent does. When the kids come home, they're only really awake for two hours. They do their homework; they eat, and then go to sleep. The rest of the night, the kid is asleep. When a teacher tells me that my three-year-old daughter is acting up or showing out at school, I believe it. When she comes home with me, we only have time to read a book, do some flash cards, eat, take a bath, and then she is asleep the rest of the night. She is not awake for the next eight hours with me. I need to trust that what my child's teachers are seeing is actually happening. I then need to try to address it the best way I can. Unfortunately, some parents feel, "Oh no, not my kid." You can't always just tell the parent about their child. Sometimes you need them to figure it out. They get upset when you tell them something that only you see. They don't want to believe it. So I have learned over time to respect boundaries and let the parents figure it out on their own.

Fortunately, I did step in at a time when he was, in fact, suicidal. He was thinking about ending his life. He was having difficulty with being a closet-homosexual. He was only a few months from graduating and it was looking like he was not going to graduate unless he started getting on the ball with his classes. Well, he did, because he trusted what I said. I told him that he should talk to his mom, and no matter what, she loves him. She brought him into the world. It may be hard for her to accept, she may be mad for a couple of days, but I reassured him that she is going to love him regardless. She is going to support him regardless. He can always trust her. I'm sure of this. It took him a few weeks, but he finally talked to her. It turned out that all the things I said were true. He said, "She still supports me. She still loves me."

Sometimes kids are so afraid of disappointing their parent(s) that they just give up and take themselves out. In the end, he did indeed graduate and get his act together. I wanted him to learn that people really love you and they will continue to love you no matter what lifestyle you choose. These are true friends. If someone turns their back on you because of the lifestyle you choose, then they weren't your friends in the first place. They didn't really care about you like they said. They were just trying to be your friend to get something from you or use you at that moment. True friends will stick with you. Sure enough, they did. When I saw him later, he ran into my arms crying. He said, "Everything is going to be fine. I'm so glad you saw me that day and just trusted me enough to talk to me."

ASSUMED FAMILIARITY

*"Familiarity must be established -
never, ever, assumed..."*

Let me keep this plain and simple. At the end of the day, children know who the authority figures are in their lives. They are the same for everyone. They also know who genuinely cares for them. If your intent is genuine, you will have a better chance at reaching them. Teachers who are just collecting a check, pastors who are playing politician or parents who are abusing and misusing their authority, are all transparent. If your intent isn't sincere and isn't about THEM, you have absolutely no chance. Children know who care. Regarding some kids, all I can say is, parents may simply have their work cut out for them, but if they take the right steps, they can have a fighting chance.

Take time to build relationships with young people. Take an interest in who they are as human beings, rather than an interest in being their "boss" or imposing your will on them. Here is the bottom line: check your intentions. I will give an example.

Teenage pregnancy is something relevant to all of our communities. If a young lady has no previous relationships or foundations for familiarity previous to your decision to initiate a consultation and reach out to her, you are fighting an uphill battle. It will seem clear to the girl that you view it as is your responsibility - or a part of your job description - and that you are obligated to say something to her. She understands this, and she will shut down. If you are lucky, she will politely do her job and just sit there and play her expected role. Why wouldn't she? That's what you are doing. Right?

Maybe you really do care. Maybe your heart is in the right place. Nonetheless, there are rules to the familiarity game. You must take interest prior to the onset of crisis. You must take the appropriate steps to build a foundation for the relationship. Familiarity must be established - never, ever, assumed. It is insulting when you approach kids with "assumed familiarity." Just as it would take you aback, it does the same for them. They might respond internally with, "You don't even know me!" or "I don't even know you!" The common call with today's youth is, "Who is you?" In other words, they have rights and you have no true rights to their trust if you have no previous relationship with them. You are a stranger to them. They have been taught all their lives not to talk to strangers, so when there is no level of trust established, it is a lost cause.

Again, establish a relationship before the crisis. How do you establish a relationship? You show interest in them. You show genuine interest. They have to intrigue you. If you are intrigued, your questions don't seem like interrogation or judgments, which can turn them away quickly. Asking them about their forms of expression versus judging or condemning their piercing or tattoo are two very different approaches.

I am genuinely interested in kids. I want to be cool, and I am not ashamed to say this. The kids are the ones who decide what is cool and what is not. My established relationship with your kid gives me an advantage when it comes to being "cool" or "hip." The kids have come to know that I really do think they are cool, and that I have an interest in preserving my "swagger" or "coolness" as I grow older. Some kids tell me that my choice of words is "old" and that I need to "step my game up." Who knows which words they will be using by the time this book releases! Because of our foundational relationship, when I ask about a tattoo or about why guys are now wearing their jeans so tight, they realize I am asking out of curiosity or genuine interest. I am doing "coolness research." If anything, they are flattered. My questions are not much different from your questions, but my purpose and objective is different.

Each parent may have many different intentions. As a parent, you may think there is something wrong with the children. You may think that they are messed up in the head. Maybe you believe they are going through a "phase." You may even think that this generation has nothing on your generation: they don't know real music; their style of dress is a "copy cat" of past styles and non-original. You don't really view them as cool. To you, they seem confused or misguided. They need Jesus. When you ask about a tattoo or why they wear their jeans like that, it comes from a different place; therefore, it is received differently. When you ask, "What is that on your neck?"

They interpret the question as, "That is foolish! Why would you get a tattoo on your neck?" or "How do you expect to get a job with that?" When you ask, "Who is the father?" or "Are you guys together?" They hear, "Who is the punk? Is he gonna marry you?" or "I can't believe you are such a little slut!"

I heard of a pastor who found what he believed to be a clever approach for one of his young members about her pregnancy. He pointed to her stomach and said, "Is this what you have been meaning to tell me about?" Her initial thought was, "Who is you?"

She was offended, because she did not have a relationship or level of intimacy with him where he could come at her like that. He just assumed he had this familiarity with her, and consequently he lost his chance to connect with her. Maybe you think that she was being unreasonable. Maybe you are thinking that she should have submitted herself to the authority of the man of God. Well, what you think doesn't really matter if YOU are the one trying to reach out to THEM. You have to play by their rules. You can go back to assuming an authoritative role if you like, but that is all it is: a role. If you love them, you will meet them where they are rather than make it mandatory for them to come up to your level. This approach will get you nowhere because it only communicates to them that you find them unacceptable. If you just approach them with love and show interest, they will be more receptive. Once mutual respect is developed, you are in the game. There is no reason to flex your authoritative muscle or position. Bullying is no longer an effective method. Don't wait for them to misstep before you say something to them. Take time to bond, because you want the best for them. Build them up, starting with where they are. When your actions say that you don't want to be bothered until it's time to regulate, save face or just do your job; then you just tear them down. Your intent is questionable to them so they shut down. When they shut down, nobody can reach them - except someone who has already established familiarity.

Establishing familiarity is comparable to hostage negotiation. I recall a movie called The Negotiator starring Kevin Spacey and Samuel Jackson (1998). As a decorated hostage negotiator, Lieutenant Danny Roman (Samuel Jackson) made a career out of disarming dangerous men who don't listen to reason; but he goes off the deep end himself when he is framed for the murder of a colleague who was investigating corruption in their department. Convinced that the Internal Affairs office contains evidence that can exonerate him, Roman takes everyone inside the building hostage. Lieutenant Chris Sabian (Kevin Spacey) is brought in to negotiate an attempt for a peaceful resolution.

In hostage negotiations, the negotiator has four primary objectives:

1. Prolong the situation
2. Ensure the safety of the hostages
3. Keep things calm
4. Foster the growth of relationships between the negotiator, the hostage taker, and the hostages.

Picture yourself as the negotiator. Your young person is the hostage-taker. What might the hostages represent? How about his or her feelings, motivation, willingness to cooperate, or anything you need for them to give up or share.

In a real hostage situation, the negotiator must be credible to the captor. That is, the negotiator must act like he or she understands the reasons for the hostage-taker's actions but must still come across as strong - not just eager to please. The negotiator can also encourage activities that require cooperation and interaction between the captors and the hostages, such as sending food and medical supplies. If the hostage-taker gets to know the hostages and sees them as human beings, it becomes more difficult to harm or execute them. This is established familiarity.

In a 1975 hostage standoff on a train in Holland, a hostage named Robert de Groot, who had been chosen for death, was spared after the terrorists heard him pray for his wife and children. Some of the hostage-takers wept, and two of them agreed to avoid a lethal shot when they pushed him out of the train. He rolled down an embankment unscathed, played dead, and then escaped a short while later. When the terrorists selected other hostages for execution, they didn't allow prayer and killed them quickly to avoid the emotional strain.

Once you establish that connection, it's hard for them to resist. Go ahead and negotiate! The negotiator's first priority is to gather information. A lot of information will come from other officers at the scene, who may have scouted the area or run background checks on the hostage-takers; but the negotiator can learn a lot from the hostage-takers themselves. Sound familiar? The negotiator must find out who the hostage-takers are, why they are holding people hostage, what their demands are, who their leader is, or whether there is more than one. At the same time, the negotiator pays close attention to the hostage-taker's responses, mannerisms and general attitude to create a rough psychological profile. This can give the negotiator some clues about how the hostage-taker might respond to certain situations - a negotiator deals very differently with a depressed, suicidal captor than with a cold, rational pragmatist.

Sometimes I feel like a negotiator. Why? Because the negotiator is NOT the person in a position of authority, he is the mediator. The commander is the one in charge. The negotiator is simply the one that communicates directly with the hostages. The negotiator gets nowhere flexing his muscle/power. He only looks to discover how he can best fix the situation. He knows that being the one in control can be seen as threatening to the hostage-taker. Be very careful to not become a threat. Your kid will shut down. In other words, your child (the hostage-taker) will hang up on you, close the blinds, and begin executing hostages, one by one.

Doc Dossman

COACH DON NORFORD
build relationship & trust

Often, as a head coach, you work with a large group of kids. There are times when you need to be one on one with those kids, especially kids that have problems. Personally, I tell a little bit about my life - things that I did right and things that I did wrong. I also communicate to them that I care about them and that I love them like they were my own children. Once you take that step, you will have to demonstrate; they are going to test you on it.

Once you demonstrate that you see them as one of your own, they will open up to you. You have to be real with them and very honest with them. Once they see that, then they know that you're human too. The kids want to put you on a pedestal. They want to make you a god. One thing I tell them is, "There's only one God; don't put me on a pedestal. I made a thousand mistakes when I was your age," or I say, "One of the reasons why I'm able to speak to you truthfully and give you sound advice is because I've seen it, I've done it, and I know the consequences." Once they see that you can relate and that you care about them, it goes a long way.

Sometimes you've got to sit those kids down and just listen to what they're saying. Yes, it's time consuming but you get to know them, and they get to know you. As you continue to do that, they feel free around you. They start talking about issues. You then get the chance to do what you need to do to make things better for them. You're gaining their respect and their trust. This is the key. Gaining their respect and trust. It's not just given to you; you've got to earn it.

A lot of parents demand respect because "I'm the parent," or because "I'm your mama," or because "I said so." I encourage them to treat it like any other relationship. In relationships, you need communication. You need mutual respect. These kids need to feel comfortable before they can open up their heart and put their cards on the table.

You (parent, coach, teacher, etc.) must till the ground like you're planting a seed. You have to prepare the ground to accept the seed. It's the same thing with kids. Prepare them so you can put a seed in them. You can't do it any other way. You can give them good advice, but if they're not ready for it, then they're not going to understand it. If you have taken the time to prepare the ground - develop a foundational relationship - you will have a better understanding of them. When they do have a crisis, you will know by the way they're acting, what they're saying, and how they're presenting themselves. They're acting in a different way around you because they want you to ask to find out what's wrong. If you just say, "I want you to run this four hundred meter race" and act like you don't care how they feel, all you've done is accelerated the issue that's attacking them. You've just made it more negative than it was before.

"You know . . . you need a license to buy a dog, to drive a car. Hell, you even need a license to catch a fish. But they'll let any ***hole be a father."

-Keanu Reeves (Tod Higgins), *Parenthood*

WHERE ARE THE FATHERS?

85% of all youths sitting in prisons grew up in fatherless homes . . .

"They become what they see," I heard a wise man say. Many of the kids I deal with from day to day do not have a father in the home. Many do not even have a male figure in their lives. Others may have one, but not one who is a positive model. To some, I am the only Black professional male they know. Coach Don Norford always tells me, "Doc, you don't realize how important it is for these kids to just SEE you! Many of them don't have a male example in their life. Especially, someone who looks like they do."

When I walk into the treatment room, I usually see the child sitting on the table and the mother sitting on a chair in the corner of the room. After a few visits, I usually learn whether the father is busy working or not present in the child's life. I can walk in and determine this by simply observing mannerisms, demeanor, communication, and confidence. It shows. I work with too many young men who are without another man in the home. After some Internet research, I learned some startling facts. The things I noticed from my personal experience were not as drastic as what I was reading.

In my experience, I have found that **many young men without a father in the home:**

- struggle with how to treat women, defy, and disrespect their mothers.
- are verbally and/or physically abusive.
- may struggle with their sexual identity (either hyperactive sexually or have trouble establishing appropriate sex roles and gender preference).
- battle with anger issues.
- lack confidence.

Through my observations, I have found that **many young ladies without a father in the home:**

- struggle with how to treat men.
- tend to be more promiscuous.

I also found that **young ladies with a father in the home**:

- have a more positive outlook and personality
- are better rounded in their perceptions.

Girls with a father in the home tend to balance their emotions by having a healthy dependence on logic. In my experience I have found that logical reasoning usually comes from the father. I see these girls deal with pressure and disappointment in a more reasonable manner.

There are many reasons that involvement in organized sports can be an equalizer for issues stemming from a fatherless home. Having access to a male coach can help provide an

Where are the Fathers?

alternative to the missing link in the home. Organized sports also add to character development.

STARTLING STATISTICS

- *Nearly 2 of every 5 children in America do not live with their fathers (US News and World Report, February 27, 1995, p.39)*

- *63% of youth suicides are from fatherless homes (U.S. D.H.H.S., Bureau of the Census)*

- *90% of all homeless and runaway children are from fatherless homes (U.S. D.H.H.S., Bureau of the Census)*

- *85% of all children that exhibit behavioral disorders come from fatherless homes (Center for Disease Control)*

- *80% of rapists motivated with displaced anger come from fatherless homes (Criminal Justice and Behavior, Vol. 14, pp. 403-426)*

- *71% of all high school dropouts come from fatherless homes (National Principals Association Report on the State of High Schools)*

- *70% of juveniles in state-operated institutions come from fatherless homes (U.S. Dept. of Justice, Special Report, Sept. 1988)*

- *85% of all youths sitting in prisons grew up in fatherless homes (Fulton County Georgia Jail Populations and Texas Dept. of Corrections, 1992)*

I understand that things happen that are sometimes beyond our control. I understand that divorce rates are high. I understand that some men choose to NOT be involved. What I do not understand is how some people downplay the importance of a man being present in the home, which is apparent in the following statistics:

- 40% of mothers reported that they had interfered with the father's visitation to punish their ex-spouse ("Frequency of Visitation by Divorced Fathers: Differences in Reports by Fathers and Mothers," Sanford Braver, *American Journal of Orthopsychiatry*, Vol. 61, No 3 (1991-07, pp. 448-454)

- 50% of mothers see no value in the father's continued contact with his children (*Surviving the Breakup* by Joan Berlin Kelly and Judith S. Wallerstein, Basic Books, 1996).

A Tribute to Good Dads . . .

I can say wholeheartedly that I have learned so much from all of you as parents, but as a man, I am most inspired by fathers. I am talking about the active and involved fathers. These are the guys that show up not only at game time, but at practices as well. I even get to spend time with them at all the doctor visits, because they are right there as well. I imagine that the child of these types of fathers either feel loved and supported or feel very smothered and is about to go crazy! From my observations, I would say it is the former.

Two dads stand out in my mind and have inspired me the most: Bill Jackson and Larry Austin. These two men have taught me more than they will ever know. I recently attended Bill's funeral and, regrettably, I did not have the chance to thank him while he was living, as I would have liked. Neither man has given me any direct advice, but each has lived by example - and I was right there taking notes!

Bill was the father of DeSean Jackson. DeSean is currently the starting wide receiver for the Philadelphia Eagles. I started treating DeSean while he was attending Long Beach Poly High School. Bill was there with his son every step of the way. DeSean stayed out of trouble. If there was one thing to say about a kid with so much going for him, he had a "clean" record from high school, college, and throughout his professional career. Many athletes of promise lose it all over one bad decision, but not DeSean. You might ask, "Why?" My answer is: DeSean's father stayed on him, encouraging him, and was always there. He was at all the college games as well! This kid had a great father in his corner and with a large family he got all the support and love in the world. There were many moments that stand out in my mind and many reasons why this kid impressed me so much, but there is one that will always leave a lasting impression: his dad.

I was always amazed at DeSean's level of self-confidence and wisdom at such an early age. I recall a conversation we had while I was giving him a treatment. DeSean was at a crossroads: he had an opportunity to either play professional baseball straight out of high school or take a full scholarship to play football at a major Division-1 program. I asked him about the major factor in his decision, and I remember to this very day what that kid said to me. He sat up on my worktable and said, "Depends on what baseball is talking about.

They have to show me something worthwhile to make me skip out on a college education."

I asked, "What kind of money would that take?"

DeSean looked me dead in the eye and said, "They'd have to at least guarantee several years and more than six figures for me to even consider it."

He then laid back down for me to resume my treatment. What? I was impressed! What kid has any concept of his worth professionally? I do not make - nor have I ever made - that kind of money. I was in awe of this kid. Do you even know your professional worth? I can't say that I do, even today. He was not talking to me as a kid with wishful thinking; he was just stating a fact.

DeSean went on to have a great high-school career in two sports, but decided to go to college to play football. He then went on to become a starting wide receiver for the Philadelphia Eagles. We are still in touch, and I am still his doctor.

When DeSean lost his father to Pancreatic Cancer in 2009, he was so strong for everyone. He maintained his composure and spoke words to encourage his family and friends. When I tried to comfort him, he actually encouraged me! I do not know exactly what Bill said or how he taught DeSean this steadfastness that showed through even in times of pressure, but I do know one thing: HE WAS ALWAYS THERE. DeSean continues to be a well-balanced young man. He knows how to deal with pressure, which he has shown

Where are the Fathers?

time and time again on the field. He understands the principle of taking care of family and being there for them. He is not delusional about those around him. He understands who is truly in his corner and treats those people like gold. Again, there are so many things I could say about this young man that impress me, but what truly sets him apart was his ever-present father, Bill Jackson.

Now, Mr. Larry Austin is another man who goes above and beyond as a supportive father. He was present throughout his son Terrence's high school career and continued to be present throughout his college career at UCLA. Larry and Bill are completely different types of men. You could tell that Bill had more of a street edge to him. He was rough around the edges and unapologetic about it. This was just Bill, take it or leave it. Larry is of a different breed. He is more quiet and reserved, and somewhat conservative. He is the type to tuck in his shirt and wear a tie if the occasion calls for it. Bill would wear sneakers to a black tie affair. I include this only to emphasize the point that although these gentlemen are different in nature and disposition, they were both successful in raising amazing sons.

Terrence Austin was the #1 offensive weapon for UCLA Football. I began treating Terrence at Long Beach Poly as well. He was another impressive, well-balanced kid. Terrence was a true student athlete. His good grades and incredible athleticism had schools from all over the country knocking at his door. I remember Terrence as a good sport and a great competitor who did not take himself too seriously. Though he possessed a surplus of self-confidence, his humility always impressed me. I have seen him maintain incredible poise during stressful times. I have seen him step up to the plate and take responsibility for his actions. I continue to see Terrence. By the time this book hits stores, he will be playing professional football in the NFL.

I could go on and on about my further observations about Mr. Jackson and Mr. Austin, but the one common denominator is simply: THEY WERE THERE AS FATHERS. I am not just talking about physical presence at home, but active involvement in the lives of their sons. If I have learned anything from these fathers, it is to be there for my son. I do not intend to take credit away from mothers, but the presence of these men is the common denominator here.

I've noticed that the most amazing young ladies have the same commonality. They seem to have the most self-confidence, the most personality, and be the most emotionally balanced. In my opinion, these young ladies are well balanced due to exposure to both a man and woman at home. Observing how their parents and role models relate to one another helps the girls relate to others of the same and opposite sex. These young ladies do not seem as needy for affection or attention as those from homes without a loving man/father. I know some incredible kids from all walks of life, but the ones that stand out are the ones with fathers around.

I cannot talk about inspiring fathers without talking about my own father, Dr. Craig A. Dossman, Sr. I have learned so much from both he and my mother. I'd like to think that I am a mosaic of each of their strengths. They are such a great pair because my mother is strong where he is lacking, and vice

Where are the Fathers?

versa. This is how it should be. We should complement one another in our relationships. My parents have passed down their strengths through training as well as genetics. My communication skills (writing, speaking, etc.) come from my father. My mother is a very sweet and gentle soul, but she knows how to stand up for herself when she sees an injustice. I posses her sweet and gentle approach when I initiate a relationship with the kids and then later, after they trust me, I grow into the boisterous personality that I am known to be. My father is a big-personality guy, so I'm sure that comes from him.

My father had to set an example for me to follow before I even had the privilege of meeting Mr. Austin and Mr. Jackson. He is a very wise and deep thinker, who has a knack for making the deep sound simple. I take pride in this ability when I explain a diagnosis to my patients. I asked my father for some seeds of wisdom for my book and found this to be an excellent point of entry. I'd love to introduce you to one of my original mentors.

Dr. Craig A. Dossman, Sr., PhD

It's your job to train 'em up!

We live in a very dangerous age. Our children are killing each other every day. This should remind us of the great responsibility parents have in training their children. Certainly everyone who has ever had a child is willing to give you his or her two-cents worth of advice. However, the scriptures teach, "Train up a child in the way he should go, even when he is old he will not depart from it" (Proverbs 22:6) A very short text, with so much to say. First, consider the words "train up a child." The Hebrew term behind "train up" comes from a word that had to do with the palate or the roof of the mouth. The original use of the term described a rope being placed in the mouth of a young horse to give it direction while the rider was breaking it in with a bit and bridle. This term also described what a Hebrew midwife would do to assist a mother in bringing about the birth of a baby. Right after the birth process, the midwife would hold the tiny baby in her arms, take her index finger, and dip it into a bowl of crushed grapes or dates. She would then place that finger in the mouth of the child and massage the gums and roof of the mouth creating a sucking response. This was done to clean the baby's mouth and to create a thirst. So behind the words "train up a child" is the idea of giving direction and creating a thirst from early age.

There are many children who are made to go to church and say their prayers and read their bibles. However, they were never "trained up." This training must begin at an early stage. This training is the most important activity that parents (plural) can ever undertake. Nothing should be more important to parents than raising their children. Anything else that gets in the way of proper parenting is not worth your time and effort if your children are not being trained properly.

Your children need you to train them. They will learn without you, but it won't be to their benefit. They will continue to grow up, but not satisfactorily unless you have your hand in the process. Most parents appear satisfied with just hoping their children turn out okay. The alternative is to take the initiative to train them in God's way. Training is not to be equated with (or limited to) discipline. It is necessary to discipline or punish at times, but training is much more. To train a child takes forethought. It requires proactive training, not reactive. It

Where are the Fathers?

takes patience and planning and, most of all, consistency and persistence. Training children is not a punishment given to parents, but a God-given pleasure and opportunity.

When my children were small (a long time ago), my wife and I decided to take them on a vacation to Sea World in San Diego, California. The dolphins' graceful somersaults and how they performed to the music fascinated me. My oldest son (now Dr. Dossman) asked me, "Daddy, how do they teach them to do that?" I responded, "Look carefully after each performance: the animal is given a fish." When an act is rewarded, it is repeated. When an act is rewarded, it is repeated! Hmmm, when an act is rewarded, it is repeated!!! That's the secret. Then I said to myself, why can't I use that same principle in training my three children? Some parents focus on preaching and their children tune them out!

Behavior that is rewarded is reinforced. When a child's behavior is negative, what should a parent do? I would recommend the WW principle. This means that when a child's behavior is wrong, the reward is withheld. Some parents do the opposite! Example: At the supermarket, Johnny asks mommy for some candy, but mommy says, "No!" When little Johnny insists, mommy repeats the reply, "No!" Then Johnny begins to scream and throw his temper tantrum. In her embarrassment, mommy grabs the candy and pushes it into his hands saying, "Take this candy and keep quiet!" Mommy has just rewarded Johnny for wrong behavior. Therefore, she has reinforced it. Since Johnny was rewarded this week, he is likely to repeat this behavior next week. Regardless of her son's screams, mommy should withhold the candy.

On the other hand, when the child's behavior is right, we should follow the RR principle. If the child's behavior is right, there should be a reward. Should the reward be given immediately or over a period of time? I would suggest that you reward immediately sometimes and accumulatively other times. Reward small children right away, and older children either way. Reward consistently at first and intermittently afterwards. Well, what are you waiting on? Get started!

The following interview was conducted between Coach Don Norford and I from Long Beach Poly, on October 12, 2009:

Don: They're getting so much on how to live from entertainers, television, and the media, you know. The things they are promoting through those avenues are totally wrong. You also have some parents who may have grown up with the same influences. This generation has definitely grown up into that, so now there's no elder information. There's no passing down of good information, of spiritual information. It's not being passed down. So what you got now is a bunch of confused kids out there. Regardless, if they have money, don't have money, have a father in the house, don't have one; they still get that information because if the parents grew up in that era, that's all they know - and it's just a vicious cycle, man. And one of the main problems with young families is the absence of fathers in the house.

I've seen more mothers buying cars for kids that got "D"s and "F"s on their report card. They got brand new cars! They're trying to cover the pain of their fathers not being there. She is trying to think like a man, "This is what I should do," because they think in their minds they are doing right and feel they are protecting them too. Unfortunately what happens is that young males get so dependent on their mothers, they think all the girls should cater to them like that, rather than them take care of the ladies.

That is a huge problem. That is why we are having all these problems. A lot of violence in our communities is over those kinds of things. The boy is hurt so bad when he gets a girl and falls madly in love with her, because he wants to be a man. If the girl decides to go somewhere else or dates somebody else, he gets

Where are the Fathers?

angry because he thinks he owns her. He feels he has done enough for her to be fully committed to him. He gets angry, envious, and then you have violence. Now you have these two boys fighting over this girl. The girl sits back thinking it's something big because she has these males giving her attention. So everything is upside down. You see what I am saying? Then, when you get a bunch of young men together, you talk with them and eventually there will be a confrontation. They all want to be respected and be looked at as a man. They are not going to let nobody do any constructive criticism about them. "I am going to be a man. I'm going to take your head off." You got this conflict going on all the time. Sometimes I just listen to them talk and all their conversation is confrontational.

Doc: Where is this confrontation coming from?

Don: It's stemming from them not having a father. They don't know it and they think that this is the way to be a man. "If I ain't got the money, I got the feelings for some." Or as far as the relationship for the girl, "I got the sexual part." And it just messes up things.

And you look at the sagging of their jeans. I just hate it. I just can't take it. For now, I understand why they are doing it: they are crying out for help. "I don't know who I am." Now, the other side of that is that by them sagging, they are saying, "I am a man. Look at what I got." Then there is another side to it: some of them sag, but deep down inside they don't want to be a man. You got all kinds of stuff going on with that sagging. It goes so far, they show their butts. They dare anybody to say anything about it. They think, "I am a man. I will do whatever I want to do. I will

81

talk like I want to talk any way I want to talk. I am a man." Everything is competition.

It comes from prison (sagging), when a guy claimed a man to be his woman. They brought it out of jail, and it is taking on a whole bunch of things - and what it's doing is destroying the male. They think they are being a man, but it is destroying them. First thing, "I am going to be a man," but over a period of time you're going to see an earring in their mouth, wearing all kinds of light-colored clothes, really tight pants. It is really weakening them now. They become real weak.

When I first saw those kids sagging. Man, they did it with pride. Now you don't see it. They are becoming effeminate. I've seen them get out the car at school with their pants already hanging down. Their moms don't say a word. Mom is looking at it psychologically, as if it's going to protect her son.

Both parents are so important. Both bring strengths to the table that the other may not be able to provide. In my community, the father is a missing key element to the nuclear family. I know that statistics across the nation confirm that this is not merely an inner city problem. And just because there is a man in your home you are not exempt from the effects of the fatherless home. Revisit the statistics on fatherless homes. You will see how this can, in fact, affect you.

Where are the Fathers?

FATHERLESS & INFAMOUS

- BILLY THE KID (19th Century Outlaw/Gunman)
- SADDAM HUSSEIN (Iraqi Dictator)
- SIRHAN SIRHAN (Convicted assassin of Senator Robert F. Kennedy)
- ADOLPH HITLER (German Dictator/Leader of Nazi Party)
- ROBERT GRAYSMITH (Zodiac Serial Killer)
- MARC LEPINE (Mass Murderer of 14)
- JACK THE RIPPER (Serial Killer)
- LEE HARVEY OSWALD (Assassin of President, JFK)
- JOHN WILKES BOOTH (Assassin of President, Abraham Lincoln)
- JEFFREY DAHMER (Serial Killer/Sex Offender)
- CHARLES MANSON (Cult Leader)
- "MONSTER" CODY (L.A. Crips Gang lord)

COPING WITH PRESSURE

"... because I have to apply pressure in order for them to withstand pressure." -Coach Don Norford

I've coined a term called the "Freshman Syndrome." I haven't paid for a copyright or trademark, but I'm claiming it now in front of everyone! Every year, a new group of high school freshmen contract it! I work with kids that dominate the age-group track scene. For those of you who are clueless about track and field, age-group track is where kids can compete at an early age, but only within their age bracket. Some of my kids were dominant, even on a national level! I recall occasions when one of my kids was the fastest 7-year-old girl or the fastest 8-year-old boy in the nation. They continued their dominance throughout junior high school, because they beat the same kids every year. When kids get to high school, they have to race kids that are older, bigger, and stronger. It is here, that these "dominant kids" see their reign come to a screeching halt! It's almost embarrassing to watch.

For the first time in a 7-year track career, they feel humiliated in front of the peers they are hoping to gain acceptance from in high school. How do they manage this newfound humility? By FAKING INJURY. Yes, I see the most hamstring injuries at the beginning of every season when there is a new incoming freshman class at Long Beach Poly High School. If they are losing considerably during a race, you might see them "pull up" as if injured and hindered from finishing. Those that finish the race will look around first and then begin to limp, look down at their ankle or knee, or grab onto the back of their leg. Some even shed tears. It is highly entertaining. As freshmen, they have yet to be properly coached on the art of faking an injury, so the entertainment continues in my office. They are also too young to know that a good doctor can spot a faker a mile away. Believe it or not, there are actual orthopedic tests just to see if someone is faking. We call it "Malingering."

So, "Freshman Syndrome" is when a once-dominant freshman realizes his or her track mortality and decides to cope by malingering or making excuses. A true hamstring injury typically heals on its own, without any treatment, in less than six weeks. When given proper and adequate care, healing time is frequently cut in half. Freshman Syndrome typically takes longer to heal.

In my humble opinion, Don Norford is the best in his field when it comes to preparing a child to cope with pressure in a healthy way. His track program at Long Beach Poly is not only nationally recognized, but world-renowned. When these kids step onto the track, there is a great deal of expectation placed on their shoulders. They are expected to be dominant. They are expected to reproduce what was done years before them. They race in front of crowds of 10 to 100,000 spectators. This is sometimes even televised. They rarely disappoint. I don't know how Coach Don does it. Well, maybe after spending the last seven years with him, I do have an idea, but whom better to pen this chapter on kids coping with pressure than the coach himself . . .

COACH DON NORFORD
Insight on Coping

When you see them come in as freshmen, they are on top of the world because they have dominated in their age groups coming up. Then they get beaten regularly, and they see that they aren't invincible. They go through a period where they struggle with doubt. In junior and senior year, they flourish and turn into the type of people I know will be just fine when it comes to handling the pressure. They handle it. I see it year-in and year-out.

One of the main things we do is sit them down and be very clear about what is expected of them. It is also important that you tell them you believe in them, and that you have all the confidence in the world they are going to be successful at whatever they do in life. You have to set high standards for them. One of my speeches to the new kids on the team goes something like this:

"I'm not going to compromise or lower our high standard. I expect you to reach this standard, but I know that all of you are at different levels. I will know what those levels are by getting to know you and communicating with you. I will help you to reach our high standard, but there is no one in here that is below average. All of you are above average, or else you wouldn't be here. I don't care about what you do in your classroom as far as you getting "D"s and "C"s; those grades are because you're lazy and not because of what's inside of you. You are ALL uniquely and fearfully made by

God, and I know there is something inside you that has to be brought out - that the Lord wants us to bring out. Once that is revealed, I will bring it out. But all of you have to be able to handle life, and that's why you're on this team. I am going to teach you life lessons.

One of the ways I will teach you is by not only coaching you, but also by giving you the wisdom that I have learned over the years. I will teach you lessons in track and then show you how to apply those lessons to your lives. I will show you how to handle pressure. It's a lot of pressure being on this team. Everybody expects you to be the best. Know that you're not always going to win. But one thing I want you to know is you're not going to be judged by how fast you run or even how slow you run. How much you're willing to sacrifice and discipline yourself are the things I'm going to judge. When I say judge, I'm saying that I'm going to correct you every time you are not doing what you're supposed to do. I will praise you on the things that you do well. I will get you to improve the things that you need to improve. That is how you will be treated on this team."

After this speech, most of the kids are thinking, "Man, he ain't playing!" I'm not playing! The kids that stay on the team are able to deal with that . . . because I have to apply pressure in order for them to withstand pressure. For some, I apply a tremendous amount of pressure; and for others I don't, because they are not ready to handle it. The ones I put tremendous pressure on learn how to deal with it. I anticipate everything that can happen in the track meet and I do the same thing in practice. The things I say to them are premeditated and well thought out. Everything I need to say to each individual child is premeditated. Even the things I don't say are premeditated. It is all thought out, based on what each can handle.

Doc mentioned to me that my approach is not much different from that of Jesus Christ - His approach to Christians and how He is testing us, strengthening our faith, and building us. We are tested and pressured to create a stronger character, whether it be through trials or tribulations. Doc is correct. It is from Christ that I adopted my model. If you don't teach the kids how to deal with pressure, they are not going to be able to handle it.

Another thing I teach (without actually saying it, because you have be careful) is to be dominant. I expect the kids to go out on the track and dominate all the events. I want them to have that frame of mind, but also to be humble. Of course, they are going to find that you win some and you lose some. But even when they lose an event or race, they learn that they have not really lost, because they have learned about themselves through the effort they put in. A loss becomes positive. Losing is sad initially, but what you learn about yourself can be used for the next challenge.

You have to know those kids. Know them like the back of your hand. And you can't let them get away with stuff. They will wear you down if you allow it. And when they wear you down and you may say, "I am sick and tired of telling this one to. . ." But you have to keep telling them. If you are being inconsistent, the kids lose out, because it is unlikely that these practices are being reinforced at home. You must also give them a model to follow. By being a positive role model, you are giving boys and girls someone to look up to. They have something to judge other people by. For example, girls can say, "Coach Don wouldn't have done this, so why is this guy . . ." and the boys can say, "Hey, Coach Don wouldn't have said something like that to a girl." You give them that role model by YOU trying to do right.

On another note, I tell them all the time, "Don't put me on a pedestal, because I ain't perfect." I will sit down and talk to them about some of my life experiences. I share some of the funny things that have happened to me in my life; all the while, I am teaching them. Even when I'm joking with them, I'm teaching. I teach all the time. Never stop teaching. You don't think they are listening? THEY ARE LISTENING, all the time. Always be ready to teach and continue building them. Build them up so they can handle the pressure. Some of those kids, you just never know who they may become.

I remember a young lady by the name of Julia Singh. She always seemed to have boy problems and girl problems. I believed in Julia, so I never let her sink to the level she would try to go to. I wouldn't accept excuses. Julia was such an intelligent girl. She would always have something going on, and I don't recall her ever running in any of the big track meets; but she was still a part of the team.

Recently, I got sick and was admitted to Memorial Hospital for 14 weeks. Julia was my RN. You would have never known that this young lady was the same girl who never won a race and who rarely ran because she always had issues. When Julia found out that I was on her floor, she

Coping with Pressure

immediately took charge and had a meeting with all the RNs. Bang, just like that I didn't have to worry about anything. In fact, I was supposed to have a roommate, but I didn't get one until the last few days when they became overcrowded, and even then they still asked me if it was okay.

She told me which doctors to watch out for. When one doc started acting strange, she jumped on it. Then, one of the RNs was overly aggressive with my catheter and hurt me. It was so painful! I never saw that woman again. I know Julia said something to her. I don't know what, but the woman stayed away like I had the plague!

There is a lot of pressure being an RN. My goodness! I saw some emergent decisions they had to make and even watched them make some decisions when the doctor wasn't even there! I would hear people coming out of the rooms, hollering and screaming, and they gotta move! By Julia being on the track team and learning how to deal with pressure, she was able to do the same as an RN!

Moral of the story? You never know who your kids will become. Just be sure you give them confidence and build their character. Make them look in the mirror at themselves. Show them that they can build themselves into something great, because you know the greatness is in them. The Lord put something great in all of us! Parents have to believe that about themselves before they can make their children believe it. Parents have to know it!

The other way you teach them how to deal with pressure is when past graduates come back to talk to them. I encourage that. They say, "This is what you have to do," or "This is what Coach Don taught me." They might be some of the kids that gave me the most problems who are now saying, "Naw, you make sure you listen to the coach." Those are the kids that know what they are talking about. I recall a graduate telling a student, "Everything the coaches said was going to happen in college did happen. Here are a few things I did to do to deal with it . . ." That helps tremendously.

When college coaches come to recruit kids from Long Beach Poly they tell the kids about their positive experiences with other athletes from the school. They know our school produces topnotch student athletes and are saying, "We know what kind of kids you are, and we are willing to offer you a full ride."

Traveling is a lot of pressure on the kids. They step out there and everybody, especially at Penn Relays, is expecting greatness. They KNOW the country is watching to see what they do, and they gotta go out there and perform in a setting like that. They learn how to handle it. There comes a time before the race when they have to handle it. You've prepared them, but now THEY have to do it. There is nothing more you can do as a coach. Then there also comes a time when they have to do it alone and not rely on the team. Their teammates can't help them now: they have to reinforce what you and their parents taught them and then put all their belief in the Lord.

Coping with Pressure

Take a girl like Destiny Gammage, one of my recent graduates. Destiny didn't have any spectacular numbers or statistics, but she was still able to get a scholarship because of the reputation of the program. They know that she can handle pressure because we travel. They know it.

I remember Marcus Anderson got into trouble at UCLA because he made a few statements in the LA Times. They asked him, "How do you feel coming out of high school and playing before 100,000 people?"

Marcus said, "Well, I come from Long Beach Poly, and my track team traveled all over the country. We ran at Penn Relays in front of 80,000 people. That is nothing new to me. We ran at Texas Relays. I can handle that pressure. It's not new. We ran indoors in New York City with over 3,000 in there. I'm used to this kind of pressure. I thrive on it."

The coaches at UCLA didn't like that answer.

I told Marcus, "I understand what you are saying, but you go to UCLA now and you got to mention them. Give them some credit. Be careful what you say."

He said, "Well Don, you always taught us to be real."

I said, "Well, you got to be wise too!"

Take a young man like him. He went to UCLA and then played professional football in the NFL. Now he is part of a big company that goes all over the world and helps people with the environment. He is going into poor countries and teaching them how to use their resources and how to use alternative forms of energy. He is as happy as he can be! He is always thanking us for putting up with him, because he was something else! But he also had a really good family and support group. We were able to fill in any parts that they didn't. He was able to handle that kind of pressure.

Marcus is going into those poor countries and knowing that what he says is gonna have a lot to do with how well the people there live. He realizes they are counting on his knowledge to help them survive. Now, that's some pressure there! So as a head coach, I must stay aware of these things at all times. I have to check myself out. Am I doing everything I'm supposed to be doing? I'm preparing these kids for life. I have to go way beyond sports. I have to go 360 degrees and not 33 1/3 degrees. I prepare them for pressure and problem solving.

Of all the things kids need to know, one of the main things I teach is how to deal with pressure and stay relaxed. I teach them how to be in full control of all of their senses, because it affects how well they perform in anything they do. You must learn how to be relaxed and flexible enough to make the necessary changes you need to when things are not going your way - and still be able to produce what you were going after. This is something you learn through athletics: how to stay relaxed under pressure. As soon as you tense up, you know you are going to make mistakes.

If you're trying to build a bridge that has to be completed in a certain amount of time . . . and [you] worry about the deadline [or] you're trying to do it [too] fast, you are going to make a big mistake and cost people their lives. If you can do it relaxed, you'd be surprised at all you can do, because now you're allowing your body to flow - allowing it to have liberty from your thinking. You can be relaxed and laid back. You can be cool, calm, and collected, under pressure.

That brings to mind Usain Bolt, who lets his body run the way it is supposed to. I don't think people know how deep that young man is. That's a deep young man. To be able to run that fast? Now, he understands that in track, you compete against yourself. There he is, getting in the blocks, and the whole world is watching. They watch you compete against yourself. Everybody expects you to do something, and you go head and do it! People look at that physical part, but I'm looking at that spiritual part. I don't know what his beliefs are, but I do know one thing: you don't affect the world like that unless God has anointed you!

Think about that. He is friendly to everybody. He gave $50,000 to a Chinese orphanage when he was in China. You get $100,000 each time you break a world record, and he gave half of it back to China! You don't affect the world like that unless you have the anointing. God has to be there, so that's what I'm looking at. He is doing what people said couldn't be done. They are giving praise to everything and everyone but the Maker who made him. They give praise to his coach, to Jamaica, to everybody, except the One who made him in His own image. It will be interesting to see what is going to happen in the future. He is so young that he doesn't even recognize what's going on. It's spiritual.

You talk about someone promoting friendship, goodwill, and peace toward mankind? That's him. He is from a little town in Jamaica. Isn't that something? They are doing all kinds of tests on his blood. They may want you to think that they are just testing for drugs, but what they want to know is how is he able to run this fast? Why is he so much faster than everybody else? How can he perform at this level and take on this kind of pressure? They are looking in the wrong place! Sooner or later, it will be revealed to him. I just pray that he doesn't get caught up with the wrong crowd - that's the usual downfall - and of course, as long as he doesn't get too full of himself. If you get too full of yourself, the Lord will humble you.

As you can see, there is much involved in this process. It takes more than a singular approach. Coach Don Norford's track record is proven. He has trained some of the most elite athletes in the country. When you compete on the elite level, you shoulder an incredible amount of pressure. We see his kids do it every year without fail. He instilled this in them while they were yet kids. Though he speaks about track & field, the message translates outside the world of competitive sports. The underlying theme is that you must be willing to apply pressure in order to teach them how to withstand pressure.

The following is a list of points to consider when training your child to cope:

Coping with Pressure

- Remember to *lead by example*. They are always watching, so you are always teaching.

- *SHOW THEM how to deal with high-pressure situations*. Be strong when things get hard at home. Maybe you lost a loved one or that close friend was diagnosed with a terminal disease. Show them how to deal by your example. Share your personal experiences with them. Maybe it was something that you had to deal with as a child. They find it easier to relate to these stories. How did you deal with this situation?

- *Set high standards for them.* Help them to understand that you expect a certain level of excellence from them. Be very clear about these expectations, and leave little room for compromise. You know that they are capable because you believe in them.

- *Continually build up their confidence.* Let them know that you believe in them. Make sure they believe in themselves. (Read the chapter called "Kids With Swagg.")

- *Know your children* so that you will be familiar with his or her stress tolerance levels. Never give them more than they are ready for. This will have a negative impact on their self esteem. This leads into the next point.

- *Teach them how to deal with fear of failure.* By loving them unconditionally, they know that your love is not attached to their success. This will prevent what has become a major stumbling block to so many of us. It is called a fear of failure. Fear of failure paralyzes so many from achieving their true potential. Maybe it's that business that you have wanted to start for so many years. Maybe you simply want to ask that person out on a date. Maybe you have always wanted to write a book? If there is no fear of failure, they won't be afraid to react, make decisions, or make a move when necessary.

- *Test them from time to time*. Do this by intentionally placing pressure on them. Be sure to be intentional in your approach. I could get in trouble giving examples here. I beg you NOT to drive them 100 miles outside of the city limits and drop them off blindfolded. Remember the golden rule; do unto others, as you'd like them to do unto you.

- *Be patient!* Everyone grows in their own time at their individual pace.

- Last but not least, *trust the principles that you have instilled in them.* Then watch them grow. You never know what they might become!

Kids With Swagg

"They say there ain't no hope for the youth. The truth is, ain't no hope for the future." -Tupac Shakur

The "Kids with Swagg" are the kids with an unlimited supply of self-confidence. Their self-image is so healthy and balanced that they don't really find it necessary to follow anyone. They are typically the leaders and trendsetters at school. They tend to have their own style and they love it whether you get it or not. Did you catch that? It's not your opinion of it that matters; it's whether you "get it" or not. Whether you "get," for instance, that their mismatched colors and clothes are intentional is your problem and not theirs.

These kids are known to be happy and charismatic. They tend to be more mature than other kids because of the time spent around adults who have lovingly invested time into their lives. These kids have it going on, and they tease me for even using the word "swagg" because they gave "swagg" its proper burial in 2007! Yes, they told me this! I defended myself by saying, "Sean 'Diddy' Combs uses it all the time!"

Do you know what they said to me? "Diddy is old too, Doc!"

These kids are focused on what is most important and the task at hand. They are not easily distracted. They are not trying to fill a void of something lacking at home (love, attention, praise, or even a hug). They've got it covered.

If you get nothing else from this book, take these gems with you:

1. Love them (unconditionally)
2. Learn from them
3. Keep family around them
4. Watch yourself
5. Be yourself
6. Spend time with them; pursue a relationship
7. Never give up on them

GEM #1: LOVE THEM

Love is really the answer. You are probably reading this book because you have this part down pat already. You love your child. But they need to understand the extent of your love. If they understand this, the other gems on this list will fall into place naturally. They need to know that they are more than adequate. If they fail, they need to know that you will continue to love them. Living up to your expectations places more pressure on them than you realize, even more than they are willing to admit. Love on them. I can't tell you HOW to love them. In all of my parental surveys, "Love on them, Doc, just love on them," is the most common response I get. Kids that feel loved tend to be "individuals." They are the trendsetters, the leaders, and the mature and reasonable kids. Loving on them does not necessarily mean giving them things or letting them do whatever they want. Sometimes it's about making a decision that is best for them, rather than one you believe will make them happy.

Never underestimate how much your child understands. They know when you love them. They know when you are giving tough love and when you don't care. Let them know that they are special and more than adequate just the way they are.

This train of thought reminds me of a devotional I read, by Bonnie St. John, based on 1 Samuel 17:38-39 NIV.

"Then Saul dressed David in his own tunic. He put a coat of armor on him and a bronze helmet on his head. David fastened on his sword over the tunic and tried walking around, because he was not used to them. 'I cannot go in these,' he said to Saul, 'because I am not used to them.' So he took them off."

Bonnie St. John's devotional:

> *Our children today are very busy trying to fit into someone else's armor - to fit in with the kings of our society and trying to pass themselves off as someone other than the unique and special person that God made them. How do we reach our children so that they could have the courage David did? If a rock star was offering his clothes, his lifestyle, and his friends to a young person face-to-face, how many do you think would have the courage to say, 'No thanks, that just doesn't fit me.' David was confident that he was loved and valued by God just for who he was: a little shepherd boy. He knew that what God had taught him in the fields, God could use to vanquish his enemies on the battlefield. I still feel awe for this young man who turned down the king's armor*

and went off to face a giant. Basically, David was saying, 'I don't need to be something that I am not.' That story inspires me to see the places in my life where I am trying to be someone else, too. What messages am I sending by the clothes I wear? The diets I start? The career ambitions I have? We need to be the example for the next generation of being enough as we are. Maybe we don't reach as many young people as we could because we are trying to teach them to wear the armor we think they should wear. We mean well, but we may be trying to fit them into our own idea of who they should be. Saul meant well in offering his armor. Instead, we could tell them that God loves them and created every one of us for a special purpose. We could be showing them how to find themselves in the Bible instead of just making them conform.

If we could teach each child to honor what God did when creating them, maybe they would not become an "Emo," a "Goth," or a "Skinhead." They might not be looking for confidence through plastic surgery and designer labels. Instead, they could become: themselves. Are you reaching and teaching our children to be themselves - a unique person created by God? Reach out and help them to explore who they really are, not just who we want them to be.

A child who feels loved is a happy child. Just like when you are in a marriage or dating relationship, happiness is a by-product of feeling loved. I learned that from one of my favorite authors, Gary Chapman (*The Five Love Languages*). The child's emotional love tank must be on full at all times. How do we do this? Learning how to communicate love is the key. Gary says that there are only five basic love languages (five ways to express love emotionally). Your child speaks a primary love language, just as you speak a primary language. I am currently communicating with you in the English language. If this book were written in Korean or French, most English speakers would get absolutely nothing out of it.

This is how some of you feel: as if you and your child are speaking two different languages. You feel that you have done all you know how to do to show them that you love them. Maybe you have bought them everything they've asked for. Maybe you have repeatedly told them how great they are. Maybe you try to show them affection, but they turn you away. This is not uncommon. The key is to learn their primary love language. If you learn to speak their language, they will understand love. It's that simple. Your job is to discover their native tongue.

The 5 Love Languages

Words of Affirmation: Words that build up, affirm, compliment, or appreciate. To a child whose primary love language is words of affirmation, negative, critical, or demeaning words strike terror in his or her psyche. Hundreds of 35-year-old adults still hear words of condemnation ringing in their ears that were spoken twenty years ago.

"You're too fat."
"Nobody will ever date you."

"You're not smart. You may as well drop out of school."
"You are irresponsible and will never amount to anything."

Adults struggle with self-esteem and feel unloved all their lives when their primary love language is violated in such a detrimental manner. Positive, uplifting, and complimentary words nurture this individual on such a deep level. You can't show love to this child in a better way. They will feel loved and accepted. This will breed a healthy confidence that will carry into adulthood. This confidence will come in handy on job interviews, during the dating process, and in any other situation where confidence is deemed necessary!

Quality Time: Giving your undivided attention (not watching TV or a movie). Many adults who look back on childhood do not remember most of what their parents said but will remember what their parents did. One adult said, "I remember that my father never missed my high-school games. I know he was interested in what I was doing." For that adult, quality time was an extremely important communicator of love. If quality time is the primary love language of your child, and you speak that language, chances are they will allow you to spend quality time with them even throughout the adolescent years. If you do not give them quality time in the younger years, they will likely seek the attention of peers during the adolescent years and turn away from parents who may - at that time - desperately desire more time with their children.

Gifts: This is a visual symbol of your love. If this is their primary love language, it has nothing to do with money but the fact that you think of them. If parents have money, they tend to buy many gifts for their children. Some parents believe this is the best way to show love. Some parents try to do for their children what their parents were unable to do for them, and they buy things that they wish they had had as a child. But unless that is the primary love language of the child, gifts may mean little emotionally to the child.

If this practice of giving matches up with a child that has "gifts" as their primary love language, we have a match made in heaven. Maybe you are this way because "gifts" is in fact your primary language as well. We tend to love in the manner that we prefer to receive it.

Acts of Service: Expressing your love by "doing things" for them (i.e., cooking a meal, fixing a bike, helping with a science project). If your child often expresses appreciation to you for ordinary acts of service, that is a clue that these acts are emotionally important to him or her.

This child tends to be a joy to the hard working parent. Parenthood is often known to be a thankless job. Much of what is done may be considered one's duty or expected. Many parents don't feel appreciated. Maybe their primary love language is "acts of service." Well, this child is incredibly thankful for everything you do and expresses that gratitude. If the parent feels appreciated, the love fest will be never ending. You are both getting what you need!

Physical Touch: This includes hugging, kissing, holding hands. If your teenager is regularly coming up behind you and grabbing your arms, lightly pushing you, grabbing you by the ankle when you walk through the room, or tripping you, those are all indications that physical touch is important to him or her.

If they don't get this at home, they will get it elsewhere. This could be dangerous. Be sure to be your child's general supplier of this love language. This is a void that you don't want anyone else to fill. The yearning for love is so strong in all of us that you would be surprised at the lengths one would go to feel love. It can put your child in compromising situations. It might be with a significant other or someone not so significant. It might be another adult. I'm sure your imagination has kicked in at this point. Be sure to be the one communicating to your child in this language. We really don't have to go into the benefits of doing this. One benefit is that someone else won't be doing it.

The key is to discover each child's primary love language. The best way to go about it is to pour on all five languages. Apply all five and watch their behavior; you will surely hit the jackpot. You just have to pay attention. As you can see there is a pattern, no matter the love language. If you love them in their primary language, they will all benefit in the same way. If you do not love them in their primary language, they will all suffer in the same way. I also strongly recommend that you read Gary Chapman's book.

Gem #2: Learn From Them

Your kids think you are stupid, that may not be the case, but the truth is...you don't know everything. The sad part is that you don't know what they want you to know. If you'd just listen, you'd realize that there is a great deal to learn from them. They know "what's up." They know why that boy on the skateboard in front of your car is wearing his pants so tight. They know why the young lady walking by is proud of her "muffin-top" waistline. Just ask them a question. See what they say. If you are sincere in your curiosity, they will be proud to teach you. If you are actually waiting to shoot them down or judge them, they will shut down on you.

You might be surprised at how much you can learn from them. They have been watching you for years. They have been listening (because you won't let them talk) for years. They definitely have something to say and know more than you think. They may be able to help you in your relationship with your spouse or significant other. They may not know about adult relationships, but they may have overheard something that was not intended for them to hear. They may have seen something that wasn't meant for them to see. They know more than you think - everything from stories of infidelity to abuse. They've heard the arguments through your bedroom wall, or maybe your spouse confides in them and they know exactly how to correct your "grown-up" relationship.

Gem #3: Keep Family Around Them

Keep family around them, or they will find a new family in the streets through sex, drugs, and/or gangs. This gem is an extension of the first one: "Love Them." Family is one of the key factors for social development and expression of self-esteem. The more family you expose them to, the more people they will have to potentially love them! Please don't let any personal issues between you and a relative prevent you from keeping family around your child.

I understand that some people (even family) have absolutely no business around your child, so please use common sense here. I am speaking of petty disputes. Get over it. Your kids need positive relationships with relatives. This has been known to be a positive factor in a child's self image and is typically the first group or team setting experienced by most people. In this setting, we discover our roles and shape our identity. Responsibility and roles are paramount to identity formation. Identity formation is usually developed first in the family setting. The family environment can help the child be a better role player in the team setting.

At the same time, a child that is missing the nuclear family can have this void filled by team sports. Relationships and personal interaction are also important to identity development. You can find both in a team setting, as well as in a family.

Ownership of roles and responsibilities are strong sources of self-esteem. This is why the team concept (sports) is so beneficial to young people, especially those in the single-parent home. A team player is a role player. The various positions on a team come with particular responsibilities, and the team depends on the player to follow through with those responsibilities. Whether it's a point guard on the basketball court, the catcher on the baseball diamond, or the goalie on the soccer field, each position carries a responsibility and is depended upon heavily. This gives a sense of duty, importance and accountability. There you go! Another reason to put your child in athletics!

Kids may not show it, but they love attention and will take it from anywhere. I'm sure that sounds maniacal too, but it's true. This is why it's best that it comes from home, rather than from the streets or some pervert. Because you are family, you get first dibs, the first crack at supplying their needs. If there is a deficit, then they need to go elsewhere.

Show them they are acceptable just as they are. Everyone wants this, even you, even your spouse. This is why family is so crucial. It's a place where we can let our hair down. It is a comfort zone - a place of unconditional love. When this model is broken, the gang, streets, or other inadequate alternatives are substituted. Street love is highly conditional, but there is, in fact, "acceptance," and no matter how mild, it is something they aren't getting at home.

At the end of the day, it's all about the love. More family equals more love. More love equals more confidence and sense of self. More confidence equals more productivity. More productivity equals stronger character. This leads to healthy adults, who in turn create healthy families.

Gem #4: Watch Yourself

Children study you from the first infantile eye contact. You are their life model. They learn to communicate and acclimate to their environment by following your example. If they don't live in a household with a large family, they do not have much for comparison. Because of this, they eventually become a mirror image of YOU. Your habits, your walk, your language (foul or positive), your demeanor (mean people have mean babies), and your temperament all mold your child into a reflection of you. They are tons more perceptive than they are intelligent, and they are far more intelligent than we all think they are.

I've learned a great deal about parents before I've even met them. When I work with a team as their official practitioner, I usually spend time and form a relationship with the athletes before I get the pleasure of meeting their parents. Sometimes I never meet them and I only have their "credible" child to paint the picture for me. The funny thing is, when I do make their acquaintance, the kids are generally DEAD ON.

One thing my father taught me about relationships is, "What you allow, you teach." When you "allow" certain behaviors, you teach that they are in fact, acceptable for that other person to do. You can apply this to every relationship you have. If you are in a romantic relationship and your significant other constantly shows up for dates late, and you never say anything, you are "teaching" them that it is okay to have absolutely no consideration for your time. If he or she is verbally abusive and you never stand up for yourself, you are teaching. If your best friend borrows your car and always returns it filthy, smelling bad, or low on gas, your saying nothing is a form of teaching. If your boss makes inappropriate comments about your body and you don't address the issue, you are teaching. If your child is disrespectful in a public place and you do not correct them, you are teaching.

The same rule applies for your behavior at home. "What you DO, you teach." Remember, they are watching your every step. If you dress risqué, your daughter will follow until she learns better. She will learn at school that "whore gear" isn't the look right now, because the 80's look and tight fitting clothing are in style. If you panic every time a stressful situation comes your way, you are teaching them how to cope. If you are physically or verbally abusive to your spouse, you are teaching them how to behave. If you are never punctual, you are starting them on a bad habit. Do you smoke? Do you get the point?

My father is a Ph.D. candidate in Counseling Psychology. He often calls me to share statistics and research that might apply to my work with kids and for this book. He shared with me a theory by Albert Bandura called the "Social Learning Theory." Much of his theory is used in understanding aggression. This speaks of those who witnessed abuse in the home. Bandura states,

"Learning would be exceedingly laborious, not to mention hazardous, if people had to rely solely on the effects of their own actions to inform them what to do. Fortunately, most human behavior is learned observationally through modeling: from observing others, one forms an idea of how new behaviors are performed, and on later occasions this coded information serves as a guide for action."

There are three principles to the Social Learning Theory:

1. The highest level of observational learning is achieved by organizing and rehearsing the modeled behavior symbolically and then enacting it overtly. Coding modeled behavior into words, labels or images results in better retention than simply observing.

2. Individuals are more likely to adopt a modeled behavior if it results in outcomes they value.

3. Individuals are more likely to adopt a modeled behavior if the model is similar to the observer and has admired status and the behavior has functional value.

Think about these principles and read them again. This information may have you thinking of a million things, but I think of rap videos and commercials. They both try to sell you something by exploiting what we value. In today's society, we value fast cars, women, money, power, and respect. The commercial will attempt to make you believe that drinking Smirnoff Ice will cause you to have a good time and put you with the "in" crowd. If you use Axe body spray, you will become an instant sex symbol to loads of attractive women.

I have an even better one for you: Hip-hop music videos highlight a certain lifestyle that is valued by the public. Many of our young men have neither a father at home nor another role model. They emulate what they see on the television screen and hear on the radio.

We see negative portrayals of Black people, especially women, in hip-hop lyrics and videos. Sex is overly promoted and women are commonly labeled as "Chicken Heads," "Hoes" and other "choice words" that my editor discouraged me from using.

Messages of violence, drug usage, and sex without consequence tend to outline most themes in today's hip-hop.

This is what they see in the videos. Trust me, they watch the videos, and you do too!

The third principle of the Social Learning Theory states that individuals are more likely to adopt a modeled behavior if the model is similar to the observer and has admired status and the behavior has functional value. Translation: Your children are more likely to adopt a modeled behavior if Kanye West, Lil' Wayne and Jay-Z are similar to your children and have admired status; drinking, smoking and sexing have functional value. Many of you don't realize this, but your children are being raised by pop, rock, and hip-hop. Rap videos have an incredible amount of influence over kids; you would not believe it.

> *"Many don't have a father at home, so T.I., T. Pain, and Kanye are raising them. These men are trying to sell records, not raise kids."*
> **- Doc Dossman**

Nonetheless, they are raising yours. This includes all ethnicities. Your kids have been some of the biggest supporters of hip-hop music over the past ten years. Hip-hop is no longer just a part of African-American culture. Have you been to a hip-hop concert recently? I have. I will tell you that I saw more White kids than Black kids.

These rappers have kids of their own. They are rappers by trade, but when they get home, they are fathers just like me. They are not teaching their children to degrade and disrespect women, to value money above all, or to glorify drinking and riotous living. Don't let your children be raised by entertainers. That is what they are and all that you can expect from them. Watch yourself, because they are watching you. Kids are simply a mirror of what they see.

I travel with a few high school athletic teams from time to time. On the road I get to share more time with the kids. The interesting part is that the parents often come along as well. I love this. I get a chance to bond with parents. We go out to eat, sit at the hotel bar, hang out in the lobby, or sit together at the games. In this time I get a chance to see the parents on a more intimate level. This is where I see "where Johnny gets it from." It works every time! These kids are mirror images of their parents. I see who the class clown is amongst the parents when we go out. That same parent has a child who is the class clown as well! The parent that is low key or less outgoing totally explains the child that seems to be the quiet kid. The way they laugh to the way they express frustration. It's all there! It is amazing to me to see this. I am in awe.

Some things we do are subconscious; we may not even know we are doing them. I got to see it first hand with my son when he was two years old. One day I noticed him walking like he was injured. There appeared to be something wrong with his hip or maybe the knee or ankle. I have a doctorate in Chiropractic, so posture and function is like breathing to me. I notice these things immediately. I am very good at examining and correcting them. I tried to observe it for a few days and not make a big deal about it, but my wife began to get uncomfortable. So, I took him and put him on his back. I went through a very thorough ankle, knee, hip, and back examination. I checked both sides. I was at a loss because I found absolutely nothing wrong.

Why was he doing this? Why was he limping like a hurt puppy? Did I perhaps miss something in my examination? I started doubting my skills as a clinician. I decided to call a colleague of mine for a second opinion. What he had to say blew my mind.

"Doc, if this was an emergency situation I might have concerns about your clinical abilities when dealing with your own precious child. But this is NOT an emergency. I fully trust that you have done all that you needed to do and that if you have missed anything, you have failed to look at yourself! Have you seen YOU? Do you know that you walk with a limp? You have had the "Presidential Obama Walk" since as long as I can remember. I am positive that your son is doing as all children do. He is emulating you. Relax my friend."

Wow! This kid watches my every move and hangs off of my every word. He puts on my shoes and walks around saying, "I'm Daddy! Look at me, I'm Daddy!" He does this when he tries to carry my briefcase around the house. He does this when he pees standing up. They are impressionable from such an early age. They study your every move. They listen to your language. They observe how you respond to situations. They watch how you interact with others and how you treat your spouse or significant other. They watch and learn daily, for years. Most people tend to be visual learners, so your actions will always speak louder than your words. You cannot employ the moniker, "Do as I say and not as I do." This does not work. They are watching you. They know your habits. They notice and pick up things that you may not even notice, like how you walk. Be careful. You are ALWAYS teaching.

Gem #5: Be Real/Be You

Children need to feel a sense of realness. They need to know that adults have flaws, struggles, and have been in some of the same situations they might find themselves in. Being real with them shows them that you are willing to be transparent. It shows that you are being "genuine." It's okay to try to speak their language. It helps them see you're attempting to identify with them and within their cultural framework; but stay true. Now there is a chance that they can trust you with their cards. Kids know. They know when you are "frontin'" (being fake or being something you are not to manipulate or bully them). They know which adults really care about them, and they will tend to respond to adults who have genuine interest rather than those who simply impose their will upon them.

They are naturally resistant because they are naturally ignorant in many things. Ignorance always says, "No." When uninformed, the word "no" offers a false sense of control over the situation. When all is shaky around people, they seek to have control over something. Just be you. Don't think you have to be something you are not. This is a problem that most kids already struggle with. God has equipped you with what you need. You don't need anything else. Oh, yes you do... love!

Remember that they are humans, not much different from you are now or once were. Finding common ground shouldn't be difficult if your heart is in the right place. When you put up a front (facade) of being perfect, they think you are trying to display what you expect or think is acceptable. You are "teaching." If they don't measure up to that perfect image you have chosen to portray, they won't even try. They will shut down.

Gem #6: Spend Time with Them

Spend time with them. It is just that simple. I realize you are busy, but we are typically busy due to procrastination or poor time management. Making time to spend with kids sends a message: it tells them they are your priority. It makes them feel special and worthwhile. It builds their self-esteem and creates an opportunity in which you can pursue a relationship with them. The quantity of time you spend with your children matters just as much as the quality of that time. Also, spending time doesn't necessarily mean you have to do anything special. All it means is that you are giving them your interest and attention.

Please don't let the television raise your children. Some of you consider time watching TV with them as spending quality time with them. Wrong! They can do this with or without you. There is no growth, connecting, or bonding watching an episode of American Idol. If your child is already a teenager and you are just now showing interest in spending quality time with them, at this point it is unlikely they share this same interest. I am hoping to help you by writing this book.

The best quality time isn't the planned-out trips. Often these are places your kids don't really want to go to anyway. They probably feel they could be doing something better with their time. Quality time is found in those seemingly mundane tasks. I'm talking about household chores, eating at the dinner table, and even daily prayer and devotion.

Quality time is very hard to come by in today's busy world. You have to seize the moment in the little things, as stated before. To add one more suggestion, think of the time spent in the car driving from one place to another. Look at this as time to strike up a one-on-one conversation. How do you do this? Hmmm . . . how about taking an interest in them? What are their interests? Ask questions about what they like. Ask open ended, rather than yes or no questions. When you ask questions that begin with "tell me" "why" or "what," you are opening up the door to conversation. Do not allow them to simply reply "yes" or "no." Ask them about their favorite movie and why they enjoyed it. Ask their opinion about various issues - political, spiritual, whatever. Talk about your day and the problems you often deal with. This will teach them problem-solving skills. Problem-solving skills help them with peer pressure, drinking, drugs, or any other risky activity. Spending time with your kids also allows you to shape their values and monitor their exposure to the strong influences of their peers and pop culture.

During this quality time, keep conversations positive. Some of you always have to slip in something negative once you get your child's attention. All it takes is a single trigger for them to lose interest in what you have to say. KEEP IT POSITIVE. Don't use this time for your platform of reform. Praise them for what they are doing right. Praise them for the small things we usually take for granted. Maybe they have been waking up on time for school during the week. Praise them for that. Try to avoid the negative. Avoid being judgmental. Take the time to establish and build a relationship with your child. Remember, if you are reading this book, you are pursuing a relationship with them - not the other way around.

As you begin to develop a relationship, you should then take it to the next level. Once they discover that spending time with you can be harmless, plan a special outing. Get creative. Start with something they particularly like first. If they like sports, take them to a game. If they compete in sports, attend one of their games. Later, you can get even more adventurous and start exposing them to things that are educational or horizon expanding. Take a trip somewhere - go out of state or camping. Plan activities that encourage teamwork, problem solving, or planning. Find something to celebrate about them during this time, no matter how challenging it may seem. You have to make it all about them. Remember, if they don't get quality time from you, they will get it from somewhere else.

Here is the bottom line: If you love them, take interest in them. When you have an interest in something, you will spend time learning about it. If you are too busy with life or you make them feel that they are not your top priority, you will regret this. Make time.

Gem #7: Never Ever Give Up On Them!

I deal with some kids who many might deem "lost causes." Some of your most talented athletes are Ron Artests and Dennis Rodmans in the making - full of talent, but seemingly hopeless when it comes to respect for authority.

They stand out as "societal misfits." Many appreciate these kids merely for what they can do on the track or on the court, but outside of sports, expectation for achievement is minimal. It is almost expected that the future is grim for these kids. If they don't make it to the big leagues, we are almost certain they will somehow end up dead in a dark alley or strung out on drugs. You know which kids I'm speaking of. They are everywhere. Some cases are not so extreme, but what troubles me is that it doesn't seem to take very much for us to give up on them.

I remember a kid who was in the tenth grade when I first met her. She was a very successful track athlete, dominating on a national level, and had even represented the United States on an international level. The future seemed so very promising for this young lady. She was being compared to "the greats" in various publications because of her talent. Her only problem was her attitude: she was known to associate with local gang members and had begun drinking and smoking at an early age. She was beginning to experiment in various levels of promiscuity, including homosexuality. Whatever you could think of, she was probably into it at some point in time. The local police officers knew her by name. Other athletes, students, and even teachers grew to fear her. Her reputation was overshadowing the athletic legacy being built. It was even getting to the ears of many big school college recruiters. She was on the road to disaster.

I remember when she first came into my office. I already knew who she was, both from her street reputation and by what she had done on the track. I knew her track record, as well as her track and field records. One of my kids brought her in because she hurt her leg while running. She was from the rival school, yet she was from his neighborhood and like a family member to him. He asked me to "take care of her." He had become like one of my sons, so I took her on as a pro bono case.

I began to treat her and developed a relationship in due time. Though I was in a position of influence, nothing seemed to get through to her. She could look me dead in the eye and appear to comprehend every lesson, but the very next day she would get involved in a fight, get in trouble at school, or end up cursing out a coach. This was happening on a weekly basis! After successfully developing a strong influence over hundreds of kids, I could not get through to her. I became extremely frustrated with my lack of progress. I felt like I was wasting my time. There were times that I drove her home and we had very deep conversations. I realized she was much wiser than I could have ever imagined, but I began to think she was taking my kindness for a weakness. I was in over my head and felt that I was getting nowhere with her.

I talked to Coach Don Norford about this situation and told him that I was ready to put my hands up in surrender. This is when he shared the following words with me:

"Never give up on the kids, Doc. Never give up! Their teachers and parents might give up on them, but we should never, ever give up. Keep talking to her. She is listening. Trust me. One day she will get knocked on her behind, and she will remember everything you told her. Some of us just need to get knocked around and learn the hard way, but she hears you! She is listening!"

He told me about how powerful she was, and how she held considerable influence over the other kids. "She is just playing for the wrong team right now. Can you imagine if she was a soldier for Jesus Christ? Do you realize how many lives would change if she used that same energy for good?"

I took this advice from Coach Don and vowed to never give up. I continued to nurture her, believe in her and encourage her. Years later, I took care of her at the 2009 U.S. National Track and Field Championships in Eugene, Oregon. I was stretching and massaging her in preparation to run against the professional athletes! The night before the final race, she came to me for treatment. We had a nice talk. She is older and wiser now, but still full of fight and still doing things her own way; I could see the growth and drive. I was happy for her. She knew that many had counted her out, but she was not going to give up on herself because she also knew there were still people in her corner.

Long story short, she made the team as an alternate. To make the world championship team for Team USA, you have to make the top-three in your event. She came in fourth in the country! She will now be going to Berlin, Germany, as an alternate for Team USA! She called me to thank me for not giving up on her. She was as happy as a little girl. She told me, "Doc, my life has changed! Agents are calling now! Shoe companies are interested in me now. The phone is ringing! I'm so happy!" I couldn't be happier for her. I am so proud! Her life is changed and she acknowledges that she can't continue doing things the same way she did in the past.

She continued to display wisdom beyond her years by how she remained grounded when she told me of the many calls coming in. She mentioned that she had decided to go with the agent who had shown interest in her before that weekend. She knew that the others were only interested because she had just shocked the running world, but she wanted to work with someone who had believed in her beforehand. This was important to her. As a consequence, her agent isn't some big name guy to brag about and is not known for his big-time athletes. He is simply an attorney who believed in her before that weekend. It is too early to know what will happen next, but I am happy that not everyone gave up on her.

Never give up on children. Kids know when you have given up on them and have deemed them hopeless. They will continue to fight as long as someone is in their corner. Let that person be you. Please!

This made me think about how the devil never gives up on us. Even if you are the pastor of a 10,000-member church and seem to be perfect or sinless, Satan will simply double his efforts towards you and attack your family. When most of us think we have a hopeless case, do we double our efforts, or just give up? Just remember that the devil will never give up on our children. Why is he more committed to them than we?

These kids represent our future. "They say there ain't no hope for the youth. The truth is, ain't no hope for the future." (Tupac) This statement is profound! He is speaking of those who have already given up on the youth of today. If they give up, they are only shooting themselves in the foot. These kids are our future, and without them there is no hope for the future.

So there you have it. A mouthful, but definitely valuable information. If you apply these gems, you will groom your child into a picture of self-confidence. Remember, the "kid with swagg" is that kid with the healthy self-image and limitless confidence. If you raise a confident child, they will become confident adults.

> # THE TRUTH ACCORDING TO WIKIPEDIA
>
> *The wiki says that self-confidence relates to self-assuredness in one's personal judgment, ability, power, etc. It also defines it as the belief of believing in you; to believe that one is able to accomplish what one sets out to do, to overcome obstacles and challenges (Peixe, 2009). How does that sound? Would you like your children to be self-assured in their personal judgment, ability, power, etc.? Do you wish children would believe in themselves more? Of course you do. Somehow I think most of us want this for ourselves.*

OFF-LIMITS FOR PARENTS

Starting today, you need to begin your campaign for respect...

This chapter is for your kids. I am not ignorant enough to think they aren't reading this when it's about them. I might come across as an advocate for the young folk, but they know that I play both  sides. I've given you straight talk, I do the same with them. In fact, I just had a long talk and walk on the beach with my sister-in-law, who is 16 years old. I recall telling her that all her issues would fall into place if she would just step up and earn her parents' respect. Our talk inspired me to write a chapter for the young people. From this point forward, I am addressing my young people.

You guys feel misunderstood? Your parents won't listen? They don't give you the respect you deserve? Well, you don't get respect on GP (general principle). You earn it. Most of you have a problem with communication. At some point, you just shut down. You got frustrated because it seemed like nobody understood. Maybe nobody was listening. Everything you said was taken as disrespectful and now somehow you are "out of control" and need to be checked. You are getting older and feel you deserve to be heard. You deserve some rights and respect, right? Well, I'm going to teach you a few tips on how to earn the respect of your parents.

It's the little things that count. Maybe you want to persuade your parents to allow you to go to college far away from home? The key is NOT to sell them on the nationally recognized programs at the school - all the brochures in the world won't change a thing. Maybe they don't approve of who you are dating or interested in? You can lie all day long about how great he or she is and it won't make any difference. If you need to sell anything to them, it is YOU. Your parents love you and even if you think they are terrible parents, one thing they feel they must do is protect you from yourself. They think you are not yet ready to protect yourself. To them, you are not ready to be far away from home. To them, you don't know anything about love or how to choose a boyfriend or girlfriend. They are only trying to save you from yourself. It is not about anything, anywhere, or anyone but YOU. Starting today, you need to begin your campaign for respect.

Pay attention to what I am about to say. It is very important. Read it three times: The age when you emotionally withdrew from your parents, is the age they still consider you to be.

Remember the day when you gave up trying to communicate with them, you said, "Whatever, it won't do me any good." That's the age when you "shut down." Maybe you shut them out three years ago and today you are 17. Well, the last "proof of life" they have from you is of a 14-year-old kid. I think you've grown quite a bit over the last three years. Don't you? It's time to show up. It's time to come out of your shell. Come out of your room. Get off of Facebook. Pick your head up from text messaging. Most of you have become withdrawn. You feel that in the last few years it has been a waste of time even talking, so you shut down and kept your thoughts to yourself. All you do is pout and mope around the house. You roll your eyes and sigh when you don't get your way, but never bother anymore to fight. You have officially alienated yourself from your family. That means you have isolated yourself from them. Their last "real" encounter with you is all they have in recollection of where you are mentally. It's time to come back, communicate and show them that you are ready to assume responsibility, and that you can be trusted. It's the little things that make a big difference.

1. Take the Initiative
Taking the initiative simply means using your power to act or take charge before someone else does or tells you to. For example, you hate washing dishes, but you know that when the sink is full, you will be called on to do them. Hmmm . . . how about you go ahead and take the initiative and knock out those dishes? You're going to have to get it done anyway. Why not get some credit for being a mature young adult and complete the jump on task? Taking the initiative in any situation is NOT expected of a child or an immature individual. Little kids are to be "spoon fed" or "babied." It's expected and it's not seen

as a problem, deficiency, or a weakness. It is just a fact. As those little ones grow in knowledge, wisdom, and maturity, there is less of a need to prod or signal them to do what needs to be done. There is a certain level of respect given to one who takes initiative. If you want to get your parents to view you as a responsible individual, take some initiative!

2. Be Thoughtful (Not Selfish)

Children are known to be self centered and selfish. Their behavior indicates they think the world revolves around them. If you act like this, you are playing yourself!! Find ways to show your thoughtfulness. I'm going to give you something to blow your parents' minds. If you drive, next time you are on your way home, call your mother and ask if she needs you to pick up anything from the supermarket before you get home. Let her know you are near the market and wondering if you should make a stop before coming home. Boom!!! I promise you, her mouth will drop! That was free. Don't trip! Now for those of you that don't drive, let me think. I got it! If you notice a particular food or drink item in the refrigerator is running low, don't be so quick to finish it! Offer it to someone else before you "kill it." Again, mind blown!!! That was for free as well. Holla at ya, boy!

3. Curfew

This one is short and simple. If your curfew is at midnight, don't come in at 12:02! Don't even come in at 12:00 sharp! Come in at 11:30 or 11:45 at the latest! Don't give your parents room to wonder if they are going to have to "get on you" as they watch the clock that night. It's not really about cutting your fun short or beating the clock; it is about working within the confines of the rules given to you. Kids are always testing their limits. When given an inch, y'all will take a mile! You want to see how far you can take it without bringing bodily harm upon yourself. If you can show you have grown past pushing their limits, things will change for you. Trust me on this.

4. Take Interest

Take interest in them (your family, parents, and siblings). I tell your parents the same thing. When we take interest in others, we show that we are thoughtful and not a self-absorbed child. People are flattered when we take interest in them and what they like. While you were busy separating yourself from your family, that alienation was taken as insult. It's an insult, and they can take it personally. It is taken as if they are not good enough or cool enough for your time. It's not exactly a way in which we show our love and adoration. If there is something that your parent or sibling would like to do with you, do it and act interested. Fake it until you make it. I promise, this act will be much appreciated and thoughts concerning your level of maturity will begin to change. These thoughts will not change because of you taking interest, but because you are giving them another shot at getting to know you. They will see you are not the same person you were when you first chose to "shut them out." Take every opportunity to sell yourself. Remember, it's not about that boy or that school or that car . . . it's about YOU. You must prove yourself worthy of their trust & respect. Everything else will fall into place.

5. Try Something Different

I like this one. This one will blow their minds as well. This one is also simple. It can be fun if you look at it like a game. Change your reactions! What I mean by this is for you to try a new response to a typical situation. You know how your loved one typically responds to certain things. You know what to expect if your chores don't get done or if you come home past your curfew, right? Well, they have similar ideas about you and how you respond. Let me tell you, most of those ideas are not necessarily positive. You have probably developed a reputation for responding to adverse situations in a childish manner. Maybe you pout, roll your eyes, or even sigh when asked to do something you don't want to do. Maybe you get a nasty attitude when you don't get your way. This is childish. Grow up! Try something different. Show that you can handle adversity or that you don't always have to get your way. Children typically don't understand that they can't always have their way; try to dissociate yourself from this perception. If you ask to borrow some money, and you don't get the answer you were looking for; just say, "Okay then, thanks for your consideration!" with a smile. If they say you can't go out to the party this weekend, don't suck your teeth; just say, "All right then, thanks for your consideration!" I know you're thinking: "Yeah, right, Doc. Are you crazy?" I know you are thinking this because you are predictable, because you are young. What you should have thought was, "Wow, Doc, you make an interesting point!" Though I am being humorous, I hope you get my point. Do something other than expected. Blow their minds! Don't break character until they look away! Fake it until you make it!

6. Come Back

Come back! You have alienated yourself for who knows how long. You keep your distance and say very little. You barely speak when spoken to, because you feel misunderstood. Everything you say seems to be taken as disrespect. You figure, "Why bother?" So you shut down and no longer communicate with your family. When all of you are together, it is beyond clear that you would rather be somewhere else. You are way gone. Come back! Let them get reacquainted with you again! Show them there is more to you than meets the eye. Show them you are mature, dependable, responsible, and trustworthy. Remember, you are selling yourself. You cannot do that while off in a corner keeping to yourself because you've got an attitude.

7. Take Responsibility for Your Actions

This one is pretty big! Little kids are notorious for the blame game. They never take responsibility for their actions. They always have an excuse and label it as a "reason," and it's never ever their fault. If you do the opposite of this, you are on your way to maturity. Own up to your mistakes. Take responsibility for your actions rather than lie or blame someone else for your mistakes. This is a sign of a mature individual. Why would I let you borrow my car if you never take responsibility for your actions? Can this person be a responsible person? NO. A mature person is typically responsible. If something should happen to my car while it was in your care, I can trust that you will be honest with me and also be willing to remedy the situation rather than run from the responsibility. Borrowing a car is a huge responsibility. Show yourself to be responsible and trustworthy.

It's on you. You must show yourself to be a mature, dependable, responsible, thoughtful, respectable, and intelligent young adult. Don't get caught up in arguing or defending a person, place, or thing. It isn't about that. It was never about that. It's about YOU. You can have a great start in the right direction if you just follow my instructions. It's the little things. Yeah, I know, what you're thinking, "That guy is good!" You're right and you're welcome.

"Our deepest fear is not that we are inadequate. Our deepest fear is that we are powerful beyond measure. It is our light, not our darkness that most frightens us. We ask ourselves, Who am I to be brilliant, gorgeous, talented, fabulous? Actually, who are you not to be? You are a child of God. Your playing small does not serve the world. There is nothing enlightened about shrinking so that other people won't feel insecure around you. We are all meant to shine, as children do. We were born to make manifest the glory of God that is within us. It's not just in some of us; it's in everyone. And as we let our own light shine, we unconsciously give other people permission to do the same. As we are liberated from our own fear, our presence automatically liberates others."

- Marianne Williamson

Sports & Character Development

"It's not just a game. It's more than a game."
-Doc Dossman

"It's just a game!"

"Why take it so seriously?"

"Who cares? It has no bearing on real life!"

I can go on and on about how the importance of sports is downplayed by parents and other authority figures everyday. I often wonder if perhaps these are the people who never excelled in athletic competition and are consequentially bitter. From my perspective, what could create a better tool for character development? All the principles one must learn to be fully equipped for adulthood and the "real" world can be learned on the field, track, or court. These are principles such as teamwork, communication, sportsmanship, discipline, self-confidence, coping under pressure, handling a loss, physical fitness, motor-skill development, planning and execution, and problem solving. If you don't believe me, check out what other people have said about the benefits of sports.

All the following can be achieved through team sports:

Teamwork

"People have been known to achieve more as a result of working with others than against them."

— *Dr. Allan Fromme*

"Team player: One who unites others toward a shared destiny through sharing information and ideas, empowering others and developing trust."

— *Dennis Kinlaw*

"Teamwork represents a set of values that encourage behaviors such as listening and constructively responding to points of view expressed by others, giving others the benefit of the doubt, providing support to those who need it, and recognizing the interests and achievements of others."

— *Katzenbach & Smith*

"The key elements in the art of working together are how to deal with change, how to deal with conflict, and how to reach our potential . . . the needs of the team are best met when we meet the needs of individuals persons."

— *Max DePree*

"Coming together is a beginning. Keeping together is progress. Working together is success."

— *Henry Ford*

"Teamwork is the ability to work together toward a common vision. The ability to direct individual accomplishments toward organizational objectives. It is the fuel that allows common people to attain uncommon results."

— Andrew Carnegie

Communication
Communication is defined as a process by which we assign and convey meaning in an attempt to create shared understanding. This process requires a vast repertoire of skills in interpersonal processing, listening, observing, speaking, questioning, analyzing, and evaluating. Use of these processes is developmental and transfers to all areas of life: home, school, community, work, and beyond. It is through communication that collaboration and cooperation occur.

Discipline
Merriam-Webster's Dictionary defines discipline as training that corrects, molds, or perfects the mental faculties or moral character. Athletics and physical training challenges the body, shapes the mind, and encourages discipline.

Sportsmanship
Good sportsmanship is simply treating others (especially an opponent) with respect. A child who practices good sportsmanship is likely to carry the respect and appreciation of other people into every other aspect of life.

Self-confidence
How a child perceives himself has a great impact on how others perceive him or her. The rewards gained through praise, completing a task, exercise, and contributing to a group encourages a healthy self-image.

Coping under pressure
To a confident athlete, pressure represents both a challenge and an opportunity to prove oneself. For others, it can be a negative trigger that directly affects behavior, health, and emotions.

Handling a loss
This can also be categorized under good sportsmanship. Losing with a good attitude, while maintaining confidence, carries over into real-life situations. This is displayed as resilience.

Physical fitness
Participation in athletics is an excellent way to combat unhealthy and sedentary lifestyles.

According to the Centers for Disease Control (CDC) and Prevention, over the past three decades the childhood obesity rate has more than doubled for preschool children aged 2-5 years and adolescents 12-19 years, and has more than tripled for children aged 6-11 years. ("Prevalence of Overweight and Obesity Among Children and Adolescents: United States, 1999-2002"; October 6, 2004) Overweight adolescents have a 70% chance of becoming overweight or obese adults. This increases to 80% if one or more parent is overweight or obese. (U.S.DHHS) Obesity directly correlates with physical illness such as diabetes and heart disease. It can also lead to mental illness and poor self-image.

Motor-skill development
Gross motor development is the foundation for developing skills in other areas. Hand-eye coordination, dexterity,

balance, and control are all encouraged with athletics. Involvement in games and sports can actually help when a child is experiencing delays in certain developmental milestones.

Planning and execution
Game planning and strategy are a major component of sports. Studying an opponent and devising a plan to work together for the common goal is good practice for real life experiences.

Problem solving
Problem solving is applied before competition, during competition, and after a loss. This tool is valuable in adulthood. I wonder if you played sports when you ask me, "What should I do with him?" or "Will you please say something to her, Doc? She seems to listen to you!"

> *All the principles one must learn to be fully equipped for adulthood and the "real" world can be learned on the field, track, or court...*
>
> **- Doc Dossman**

I could go on, but it would be overkill. Can you name ONE activity in which a child can gain so much? Musical-talent development could possibly take a distant second place; however, this provides mostly cerebral stimulation with very little physical development (other than fine motor skill). Sports are pivotal, yet underrated, in child development. However, problems arise when balance is lost. The beautiful potential of the student-athlete can never be realized when a parent, coach or child places too much emphasis on athletics and not enough on academics.

My world of youth sports is very interesting. I deal with the pride and joy of the parent. No matter how talented their child is or not, "My child deserves to be a starter." Everyone has birthed an awesome and unstoppable athlete. I see the parents take their children's competitions to another level of seriousness. It is no longer about character development but about winning, praise, and self-glorification. It is about bragging rights for parents.

I see parents gain "sideline social status" amongst the other parents based on the level of play by their child. I also see the parents whose child does not excel as much as the others have their "social stock" plummet after a single poor performance! Are you kidding me? We have got to refocus on character development. The kids who are the weak links should be embraced and nurtured rather than chastised. The physically inferior athlete isn't necessarily inferior in character. I know of many teams where the stronger teammate has a weak character. This child's parents have invested time and money into their physical/athletic prowess. They have hired people like myself, personal trainers, private coaches, and more to give their child a chance to be the very best. This is all well and good to be supportive, but the motivation must be checked. Breeding superior athletes might pay off when the goal is a free college education, but social status should never be the focus for either the child or the parent. Try to ensure your child gets a well rounded experience when involved in competitive sports. Make sure they learn how to celebrate victory as well as accepting defeat and dealing with a loss. These lessons are also key to character development. Playing on a team with players of lower skill level helps better develop their own skill and teaches them to help others. It allows them to invest in the betterment of others, rather than talking bad about them on the sidelines like many of their parents who clearly have not learned this lesson.

I love to see the parent who takes their 12 year old child's game seriously like its a professional competition. You would think they were getting paid. They yell and get upset with the referees. They campaign to have a coach fired when they don't put their kid on the court/field or win enough games. You wouldn't believe the things that I hear and see. The pressure these kids have to deal with is relatively high for a child's game. When it's all about winning and stomping out the competition, character development is sacrificed. When it's all about pointing out and exploiting the weaknesses of your opponent and even your own teammate, character development is sacrificed. It's all about character development, otherwise it's just a game. I am here to tell you that it is not just a game. It's more than a game.

There is nothing like a student-athlete; a balanced and healthy individual with things to do! They can apply all the character development principles learned in sports to their academic pursuits. It works! Kids that do not participate in extracurricular activities may not be as healthy or as balanced, and have nothing but idle time on their hands. Maybe they choose to devote this time to their studies. Maybe it is time spent in the streets. Is a well-balanced individual being developed in either scenario? Is a straight-A, unbalanced student more desirable by colleges? No. Colleges recruit the students who are well rounded and balanced. This type of student handles the pressures of college life successfully. This student demonstrates the well-balanced character development previously described. Being "book smart" is not synonymous with being smart about life.

One of my clients, Brianna Glenn, is one whom I would consider to be a perfect model of the student-athlete. While attending the University of Arizona, she won two Pac-10 titles in the 100- and 200-meter sprints, and two NCAA titles in the 200-meter sprints and long jump. Her national titles in the long jump and sprint events were a combination that made history. She was also an excellent student! She earned All-Pac-10 Academic first team, GTE/CoSIDA Academic All-District VIII second team honors, and was the 2000 Mary P. Roby Academic Achievement Award winner. I follow her blog periodically as she travels the world as a professional track and field athlete. One entry reiterates this point exactly. After reading it, I immediately text messaged her for permission to include the entry in this book. She happily said, "Of course." See what she wrote about how participating in sports has affected her life.

Sports & Character Development

BRIANNA GLENN, USA TRACK & FIELD

"Life Lessons"

excerpt, August 11, 2009

www.mysocalledfabulouslife.blogspot.com

Yesterday in the weight room, one of my training partners looks at me and says out of the blue, "Isn't it weird that you thought you might not even be able to compete this year?" Yes, weird. But also . . . inspiring. A quick look back through the archives (one of the benefits of blogging, I might add) shows just how unsure I was about this season and my ability to make anything out of it. I was literally taking a gamble and hoping I could just find a way for my body to hold up and allow me to compete. Jump or Sprint? Either one was fine with me; although I was told sprinting would be the easiest with my current problems. Jump off the right leg or left leg? I've been jumping off the same leg for 15 years and figured it might be difficult to switch, but I was willing to give anything a try. So jumping it was, off the opposite leg no less, because God is funny like that.

I think that is why this season is so special for me. It's not just the idea of making a team or doing well so far and in the weeks to come . . . it's the doing so in spite of the odds against me. And certainly not in the way of proving people wrong who didn't think I was capable of doing much and should just move on, because that never is my motivation, but continuing to believe when I had plenty of very good reasons not to. In that sense, I feel like I inspire myself in some small way. (Is that even possible?) And this is not giving myself some huge pat on the back, because I will always give glory, honor, and credit where it's due. God gets it all. It's merely my job to point out how awesome He is and what a good job He's doing.

But the cool thing about sports, and something I will definitely make use of when it's time to convince someone to hire me, is that the life lessons you learn are profound and the character traits you build are immeasurable. Yes, I'm participating in a sport, but I'm also molding my character and figuring out what I'm made of. And sure, life is going to teach you that regardless, but sometimes I feel like I've been on the fast track. I have always been a confident person, but I've had to really test that assurance and self-belief over the years, as well as learn how to build it back up. (Which is no easy task, let me tell you). But when I do look back and see all the low points, it makes me that much more grateful for the high ones. It's at those forks in the road when you make important decisions and continue to add to you. I look at who I am now, and compare it with who I was ten years ago, and see such a huge difference. OK, sure, there was going to be differences simply by growing up and disregarding fashion trends that are no longer trendy. But there are still things I can link directly to Track and Field. What I understand about perseverance . . . how to be resilient . . . the importance of confidence that . . . does not change simply because of a bad performance . . . understanding what it means to really want something . . . knowing what you are willing to sacrifice to achieve it . . . believing in yourself even when you might be the only one who truly does . . . goal setting . . . setting new goals once you achieve those ones . . . desire . . . living your life so that you have no regrets . . . understanding that the journey is sometimes far more important than the destination . . . I could go on and on. But I do know this: when I look back on my life and see the person I am, there will be much that I attribute to these years. It's inevitable.

RED OR BLUE PILL

"This is your last chance, after this there is no turning back. You take the blue pill. The story ends. You wake up in your bed & believe whatever you want to believe. You take the red pill. You stay in Wonderland & I show you how deep the rabbit hole goes. Remember, all I'm offering is the truth. Nothing more." -Morpheus (The Matrix)

Please understand that I am not Morpheus. This is not the Matrix. There is no red pill. There is no blue pill. The only thing I offer is a hard dose of reality and these suggestions. Reality is the hardest pill to swallow. If you take the advice given here, you are merely headed on the right path, in the right direction. Give things time. Some healing will take longer than others. Some of you will be attempting to undo a lifetime of damage. It didn't take one night to get where you are today, and it won't take one night to get you where you want to be in the future. Just keep trying. You will find that it will take time to earn back lost trust or respect. It will take time to build a relationship from scratch.

My advice is to read the book again and take notes. Then go read Gary Chapman's book, *The Five Love Languages*. Please realize that I could not cover every single "teen issue" in this book and that I did not set out to solve every problem. I have tried to stay within the confines of what I have experienced.

This book is based on my experience with kids (most of whom live in the inner city). The kids and I have dealt with many complex issues. I call the issues "complex" because there is rarely just one to deal with. You will find that many of these topics overlap one another. Many issues stem from other issues. The topic of neglect is a major issue and leads to self-esteem issues. Self-esteem issues lead to poor choices when it comes to sex, drugs, and many other crucial life choices. These are just a few examples of overlapping. It is imperative that you find the key source of the problem. If you get the most important points of the book, you will see everything else fall into place. These points are highlighted in the chapter "Kids with Swagg." Along with the never-ending quest for open communication, those seven gems (love, learn, family, watch, be you, spend time, and never give up) will change your life.

I know a mother, who read my book and eagerly went home to apply the principles she'd learned. A few weeks later, she came to me distraught because things didn't seem to be looking up. I told her to give it time. You may have made changes and maybe even apologized, but you can't expect to develop trust and build a new foundation overnight. You are salvaging or forging a relationship that will, hopefully, grow for the remainder of your lives. Just keep working. The kids need to know that you are serious and not just "talking."

For Kicks

I thought I'd do a few things in this final chapter just for kicks. Maybe I was hard on you (pretty much during the entire book). This chapter is to end things on a softer note. Here's a little water to help you swallow that pill. I found the most interesting patterns when I conducted my interviews. In addition to my connection with various schools and athletic programs, I also have about 1,200 Facebook friends. These resources have come in handy for my surveys. You would be surprised how many parents are on Facebook. Well, I take that back. You probably have a page yourself! (My parents have a page). Anyway, this was a great way to get feedback about the book and get some questions answered. When I polled parents for their questions, I learned that most of you share the same concerns. I learned that nobody really has it all together, and that the parents with the standout or outstanding kids have the same questions and concerns as the parents of the wayward kids.

It seems that kids have the same issues, and the parents have the same questions, so I thought this would be a cool place for a frequently asked questions (FAQ) session. Here, we will entertain various questions from parents and young people from all over the country. It will be fun. You can even have your questions answered without even asking. If you see there is a question that is not addressed, visit the website or send me an email.

A FEW QUESTIONS AND TOP 10 RESPONSES

Name the top ten things your parents have done TO YOU that may have impacted your life in a negative way.

1. *Rarely heard "I LOVE YOU" while growing up.*
2. *Divorce/father was not part of my life.*
3. *Parents staying together for the sake of the kids.*
4. *Lack of communication (about sex, drugs, and other things we had to learn for ourselves).*
5. *Overprotective; controlling.*
6. *Parent said that I would never amount to anything.*
7. *Comparing me to my brother/sister.*
8. *Trying to be my friend and not a parent.*
9. *Getting "dropped off" at relative or friend's house too frequently.*
10. *Spoiling me.*

Name the top ten things your parents have done FOR YOU that have impacted your life in a positive way.

1. *Being supportive in my education as well as athletics.*
2. *Making sacrifices so I can have what I need.*
3. *Never giving up on me even though I had.*
4. *They had high expectations of me.*
5. *Teaching me to stand for what I believe in.*
6. *Father has shown how a man should treat a woman.*
7. *Single mother working hard to support me.*
8. *Raising me in a family and church environment.*
9. *Parents set a good example for me to follow.*
10. *Disciplined me so I knew right from wrong.*

Name the top ten things that you have done to cause hindered progress in your relationship with your parents.

1. *I regret all the lying and sneaking around.*
2. *I shut them out, especially when I was upset.*
3. *I was selfish.*
4. *I didn't communicate due to fear of disappointment.*
5. *Being ungrateful.*
6. *Being disrespectful.*
7. *Doing things to hurt my parents out of spite.*
8. *Being uncooperative when I was frustrated, though I wish I could have just said how I was feeling.*
9. *Choosing to maintain relationships with the wrong crowd.*
10. *Being defiant even when I knew I was wrong.*

The following are the top ten questions submitted by concerned parents and answered by young people:

1. What are some of the things that you feel your parents have done (or are doing) that negatively impact your life?

"Staying together for the kids? Why? I really feel that this has negatively taught me how love is supposed to look between two people."
- Kerry, 17, Cleveland, OH

2. Do you take responsibility for any of your problems with your parents?

"Yes, I do. I know that I shut down when I get angry or frustrated. That doesn't help anything. I know that."
- Jordan, 16, Long Beach, CA

3. What are you most grateful for from your parents?

"Moms was a hustler. So without a father, she did it all. I looked and learned from her. That made me a better man."
- Travon, 19, Jackson, MS

4. Do you think you should be included in setting the rules as well as punishments? (Clearly parents are not sure about the appropriateness or fairness of their punishments).

"In my childhood years, I didn't know any better; so I think parents must make that decision. As I got older? Yes, absolutely! Maybe beginning at about age 16, because at that age, I understood more and could have even suggested punishments that would have been helpful. Spankings after the age of 16 were really worthless. It was like they were just taking out their frustrations on me. It wasn't very productive and it isn't productive for every kid."
- Shana, 17, Los Angeles, CA

5. What are your expectations of your parents?

"I expect them to be supportive. I expect them to be role models. I expect them to come to school events and participate as a parent when it comes to my extracurricular activities, including basketball. Just having someone in those stands clapping and cheering goes a long way. I expect my

parents to raise me the best they know how, so that I can be an outstanding adult and find my own way in the world."

– J.D., 15, Oklahoma City, OK

6. What do you feel are your responsibilities as the child?

"My responsibilities as the child are to go to school and use the tools they've given me to go out and chase my dreams in this world."

– Charlie, 14, Long Beach, CA

7. Do you feel your parents love and appreciate you? If not, what can they do to show you otherwise?

"How can I feel that way when they never say those words to me? We don't even talk. Sometimes I feel they are trying to live their basketball dreams through me when they push me so hard, though they say they are hard on me out of love. They can start by simply saying that they love me."

– Terrance, 17, Los Angeles, CA

8. If you got a guarantee that your parents would not get upset, what one thing would you tell or ask them?

"First of all, that I like girls. I was involved with a female who ended up getting pregnant while we were separated (because I was cheating) but we worked it out and I decided to stay with her. I played a part in that child's life and when things didn't work out between us, she stopped letting me see the baby. I was in so much pain, but I tried to hide the hurt because I felt as though nobody would understand why I was so

upset and hurt. I loved that child as if it was my own, and I fought so hard to try to be a part of his life. I was changing diapers and getting up at 2 a.m. making bottles! But being only 18 years old, people already looked at the situation as if it were messed up anyway, because I was young and it was someone else's child. Well, to this very day I miss and love him so much! Now he's about to be two and he can do all the cool stuff. He can walk, talk, play . . . I'm not even there to see it."

- Katrina, 18, Long Beach, CA

9. Where are you in your personal spiritual walk?

"As far as the spiritual walk . . . I haven't learned to love God for myself, just outta force . . . so at this point if I were to be put on my own, I don't think I'd care enough to get closer to Him. Not so much I'd stray away, but church with mom and dad hasn't left the best impression. I wish I didn't blame them for my distance from God. I know that I am supposed to take responsibility for my own actions, but this is where I am."

- Brian, 17, Westchester, CA

10. Do you think that you can talk to your parents about anything?

"No. Mom goes through the motions as if she hears, but she does not listen. She is so quick to jump to conclusions. Communication is already bad enough. Plus, she isn't the most open-minded person."

- Angel, 16, Memphis, TN

Red Pill or Blue Pill

I hope you find this compiled list helpful. Maybe the answers were not helpful. Maybe the various answers were extremely helpful. The point I'd like you to appreciate is that everyone struggles with similar issues. It's very likely that you can identify with some of the questions listed. You are not the only one. Please find comfort in this information. Most of the kids follow similar patterns so learning from the listed issues and concerns might be helpful for you.

The intent of this book is to share what I have learned from kids. I got this stuff directly from their mouths. It is not from my "religious observations or opinions." This is live and direct from them. I have made it very clear that I am God-fearing and Christ-like in my approach to children, but this book is not about me. It is neither about my upbringing nor about what my parents have taught me.

I've heard quite a bit from religious fanatics who feel that I should have included a more Bible-based approach. In my opinion, you can find plenty of books like that at the local Christian bookstore. Maybe my approach sets this book apart from others. I have taken the approach that Christ took. He wasn't a Bible slinger. He saw a need and He met it. If you needed food, healing, or freeing from demons, He ministered to the need. When He spoke, He was very practical and spoke in parables so that His points were well illustrated and easy to understand. Godly principles were applied and, exposed to those who desperately needed to hear His messages. Some people might be turned off by or walk past the religious books, but practicality reaches them.

I don't just want this book to be a reality check or a slap in the back of your head. I only want to show you the things that I have learned from hundreds of kids. Maybe you don't find them to be credible because, "They're just kids."

You can choose to throw this book away and be angered at the loss of time you can never get back. Some of you might take this all to heart and may be paralyzed with guilt. Maybe you think, "I've screwed up my kid so much, I should just give up!" However you feel about the impact this book has made on you, it was written to open your eyes and call you into responsibility.

This book is not meant for discouragement. I want to encourage you. Most of all, I want to encourage you to never ever give up. There is so much more at stake than what we can see with our own eyes. I love these kids and would not have shared this with you if it weren't going to be a positive contribution to their lives. If I just beat up on their parents and then walk away, I just make matters worse. I am not here for that. I love them too much for that.

I want you to take the next step and begin the healing process. I'm not sure where you are personally with all of this, but maybe you need to seek forgiveness (and most of all forgive yourself). Maybe you need to apologize to your child and try for a fresh start. Maybe you see that you and your family might need counseling. Do something. Make a change. Don't keep doing the same things, expecting different results.

You don't know the plan that God has for these kids. You might have the one who will cure AIDS or cancer or sickle cell anemia. You might be raising a Nobel Peace Prize winner. Your child's invention might save lives or bring happiness and joy around the world. Your child might be the one who will one day save your very life. Be careful how you handle God's children. Nobody is a waste. Everyone was put on this earth for a purpose. Whatever that purpose is, there is nobody on this earth better qualified to carry it out. I hope this motivates you to pick yourself up, dust yourself off, and get back in there and fight for your child!

> *"I believe the children are our future.*
> *Teach them well and let them lead the way.*
> *Show them all the beauty they possess inside.*
> *Give them a sense of pride to make it easier.*
> *Let the children's laughter remind us how we used to be . . ."*
>
> — Whitney Houston

Slang Dictionary

"Remember . . . Communication is Key"

One more thing! I would like to suggest that you learn some of their lingo. I am not encouraging you to start talking like them. Please don't play yourself! I am encouraging you (once again) to take an interest! Some of you actually think you know, but you really haven't a clue. Below is a list of words commonly used by your kids today. Realize that some words are regional or even cultural. Kids on the East Coast speak differently than those on the West. Even kids in Northern California use different lingo than those in Southern California. This is the bonus section. It's not that deep, but it could be fun for everyone. Imagine the look on their faces when you use one of their words!

* * * *DISCLAIMER* * * *

PLEASE UNDERSTAND THAT MOST OF THESE TERMS HAVE A SHELF LIFE; SOME ARE USED LONGER THAN OTHERS. I CANNOT GUARANTEE ANYTHING ON THE LIST BECAUSE IT IS HIGHLY LIKELY THAT BY THE TIME YOU READ THIS BOOK, SOME OF THESE WORDS WILL BE OUTDATED AND IRRELEVANT. NONETHELESS, THIS IS A POINT OF ENTRY FOR CONVERSATION. DON'T TAKE YOURSELF SO SERIOUSLY. LET THEM TEASE YOU FOR TRYING TO BE COOL. LET THEM JOKE WITH YOU ABOUT YOUR LATENESS AND USE OF RETIRED SLANG. IT'S POSITIVE COMMUNICATION. REMEMBER: COMMUNICATION IS KEY!

WEST COAST SLANG

10 on a 2 - exaggerating (big time)
"He thinks the Clippers are gonna make the playoffs. I told him he was putting a 10 on a 2."

bananas - unbelievable, crazy, nuts
"Man, have you seen the trailer for The Orphan? That movie is gonna be bananas!"

beasty - killer, dominant (sports lingo)
"Kobe's skills are beasty on the court. Kobe is a beast."

becky - oral sex (performed on a guy)
"Hold up, you mean to tell me she gave you that becky?"

boy/girl stop - be quiet (originated in the south by Big Boi from Outkast)
"Boy stop!!!!"

burnt - said to you when you say something stupid
"You are burnt out."

buster, mark - a punk
"You know what man; you are acting like a lil buster right now."

Slang Dictionary

chicken head - A FEMALE WHO LIKES TO GIVE ORAL SEX
"PLAIN AND SIMPLE, I DON'T MESS WITH CHICKEN HEADS."

doo doo mama/daddy - FEMALE/MALE THAT IS NOT CUTE
"EWWW, LOOK AT THAT DOO DOO MAMA!"

dusty - DIRTY
"YOU WILL NEVER CATCH ME IN NO DUSTY SHOES."

faded - DRUNK OR HIGH
"I AM TRYING TO GET FADED TONIGHT AND PASS OUT!"

fasho - FOR SURE
"I AM GOING TO BE THERE, FASHO!"

function - PARTY
"AYE, COME TO THIS FUNCTION WITH ME."

geeked up - EXCITED
"I HAVEN'T BEEN OUT IN SO LONG. I AM SUPER GEEKED UP!"

go hard in the paint - TO GIVE 110%, DO IT BIG, NOT LETTING UP, USED WHEN DOMINATING A COMPETITION
"I GO HARD IN THE PAINT!"

go play, bye boy/girl, gone - GET OUT OF HERE WITH THAT MESS
"WHAT? GIRL, GO PLAY." "WHATEVER, BYE BOY. GONE!"

hella, hecka - extra, super
"Them new jeans is hella tight!"

high key - for real
"Jay-Z is the greatest of all time, high keeeey!"

jerkin' - that's tight
"Man, those shoes are jerkin'."

kick rocks/fall back - to leave a situation
"C'mon man, kick rocks."

low key - for real, quiet as kept
"You may not have thought about this, but . . . That club was fun low key!"

max poppin' - overly exciting
"Marcus told me that Drake's new song is max poppin'!"

mickey - crooked, weird
"Man, your brother is mickey for talking to Alanya."

mula, gudda, gwuap - money
"I gotta go to work and get that gudda!"

O.C. - out of control
"That party was O.C."

on deck - readily available
"On the weekends, I keep that Ciroc on deck."

Slang Dictionary

outta pocket - WRONG FOR THAT
"MY FRIEND ALWAYS TELLS ME I AM OUTTA POCKET, BECAUSE I DON'T LIKE HIP-HOP MUSIC."

pop - TO HAVE A GOOD TIME, PARTY, CELEBRATE
"WE GON POP TONIGHT!!"

ratchet - A REAL STANK MALE/FEMALE; TOO MUCH, WILD
"THOSE FEMALES IN HURRICANE CHRIS' VIDEO WERE RATCHET."

shaded - TO STAY HOME OR RELAX
"I AM NOT GOING ANYWHERE TONIGHT. I AM SHADED TONIGHT, BRO."

sketchy - UNTRUSTWORTHY
"I DON'T KNOW IF I TRUST THOSE DUDES. THEY SEEM SKETCHY."

straight drop - FOR REAL
"THEM NEW JORDAN'S THAT ARE COMING OUT ARE TIGHT . . . STRAIGHT DROP!"

swagg - STYLE, AURA, ATTITUDE, PRESENCE
"KANYE'S GIRLFRIEND'S SWAGG GOES HARD IN THE PAINT."

that's what's up - THAT'S COOL
"SO YOU'RE COMING TO THE FUNCTION? COOL, THAT'S WHAT'S UP!"

thirsty - overly anxious about something or somebody
"I hate when guys are so thirsty over girls."

tip drill - girl with a big butt, not good looks
"She is nothing but a tip drill."

toot it & boot it - to have sex with someone and leave him or her
"Jasmine is upset because she feels that Kyle got with the ole toot it and boot it."

trill - real, true, the truth (also a southern term)
"That dude Doc Dossman is trill!"

tuff - real hard/intense (somewhat flattering)
"Keisha be on me tuff!"

turnt up - high, drunk, inebriated; also means poppin'
"Man, we went to that party last night and got turnt up!"

weak - not worthy, something you dislike
"Your game is weak"

what's good with you bruh/bro? - How are you?

what's really good? - What is going on?
"You're staring real hard man, what's really good?"

Slang Dictionary

EAST COAST SLANG

badd - A REALLY SEXY FEMALE
"SHAWTY AT THE BUS STOP IS LOOKIN' BADD."

becky - KISS (DC/MARYLAND)
"SHE GAVE YOU A LIL BECKY."

beat - NOTHING TO DO OR DOING NOTHING
"I'M JUST OVER HERE BEAT. . ."

Beloved, Big Bro, Cuz, Homie - SALUTATION NAMES
"WHAT'S GOOD, BIG BRO?" OR "WHAT'S GOOD, BELOVED?"

big backin' - CHILLING WITH YOUR HOMEBOYS
"I'M JUST BIG BACKIN' WITH THE HOMIES."

bird - CLASSLESS, OBNOXIOUS FEMALE, TOO MUCH ATTITUDE
"THAT GIRL OVER THERE STAY ACTIN' LIKE A BIRD."

bitchassness - MOSTLY USED FOR GUYS WHEN THEY DISPLAY FEMALE QUALITIES (USED AS AN EXCLAMATION)
"THAT'S SOME REAL BITCHASSNESS!"

cake - EITHER MONEY OR A GIRL WITH A ROUND BUTT
"YO, I'M TRYNA STACK MY CAKE UP AFTER I GET THIS JOB."
"DANG YO, SHE GOT CAKES." (AS IN A BIG BUTT)

deadass - for real, really
"Deadass tho, that skirt looks ugly on you."

deaded - to get played, shutdown
"That girl just deaded him HARD!"

fake wilding - acting tough when everyone knows you are not going to do anything
"That kid is always fake wilding."

flow - a male/female friend with benefits, no strings attached
"I got mad flows out here."

g-mackin' - chillin', hanging out
"Last week I was just out in Queens G-Mackin' wit the fam."

good bread/good mula - as in feeling fine, okay, etc. For example, if someone asks, "You want something to eat?" The other person would say, "Nah, I'm good bread."

hubbii/wifey - a girlfriend/boyfriend (that's a real keeper)
"Yo, she's wifey material."

jack - phone
"Hit me up on the jack, I'm out."

Slang Dictionary

jonk - GIRL
"You must not know, Tramaine stay with a bad jonk on his team."

live - HYPE, FUN
"That party last night was live!"

ma - USED TO GET THE ATTENTION OF A FEMALE THAT YOU WANT TO GET TO KNOW.
"Yo, ma! Can I talk to you for a min'?"

mean mug - UGLY FACIAL EXPRESSION
"Yo, he got the mean mug on."

mixy - FUN, EXCITING
"That party last night was mixy."

mucking - HIGH OFF OF A DRUG
"Yo, I was mucking last night."

pardon self - USED INSTEAD OF SAYING "EXCUSE ME."

pop - A GIRL/BOY WHO SLEEPS AROUND/HAS SEX WITH VARIOUS PEOPLE.
"Ewwww! That girl Keisha is a pop!"

poppin' odee - SOMETHING COOL, BUT MORE THAN COOL, LIKE TEN LEVELS UP!
"Yo, ya shirt is poppin' odee."

re-re - idiot
"Look here re-re you don't know what you are talkin' about."

shorty a good look - as in your girl looks nice, very pretty, beautiful, etc.

slayyed - usually said after someone gets played or is dissed/disrespected.
For example, someone would say a joke about you then at the end say, "slayyed."

smacked/ saucy - drunk
"Yo, we bouta get smacked/saucy tonight."

smackin' - delicious
"Man, Coldstone Ice Cream is smackin'."

somethin' lite - easy, like it's nothing to me (usually used as an expression)
"I just made like 400 cash . . . you know, somethin' lite."

son'd - to punk/disrespect someone
"Ooooh, he son'd you!"

spread - money
"You got spread?"

straight cheese - no lie

"I WOULD NEVER DO SOMETHING LIKE THAT, STRAIGHT CHEESE."

tite - ANGRY
"AHHH! YOU JUST TITE THEY TOOK YA JACKET."

trills - USED INSTEAD OF "THAT'S WHAT'S UP"
"SO YOU'RE COMING TO THE FUNCTION? AIGHT, TRILLS!"

tuff - SOMETHING COOL
"YO, THAT CAR IS TUFF!"

watz shakkin' / watz roccin' - WHAT'S UP, HOW ARE YOU
"WATZ SHAKKIN' HUN?"

wavy - TO FEEL GOOD, RIGHT; TO BE STYLISH; TO POSSESS SWAGGER
"I'M SO WAVY, EVERYBODY WANTS TO COPY ME."

where they do dat at! - AN EXPRESSION USED AFTER SAYING SOMETHING THAT'S NOT COOL (TAKEN FROM THE SONG "THROW IT IN THE BAG," BY FABOLOUS AND USED BY BOW WOW, ALSO SOUTHERN)
"CHICKS THAT ARE SENIORS TRYNA G-MACK WIT FRESHMAN. WHERE THEY DO DAT AT?"

word is bond - AKA, "PUT THAT ON YOUR HOOD" OR I PROMISE OR I SWEAR
"I DIDN'T DRINK THE LAST OF THE O.J.! WORD IS BOND SON!"

wylin' (wildin')/buggin' - to be going crazy, out of control

"This morning the bus driver was wylin' out on some lady."

AFTERWORD

A concluding section in a book, typically by a person other than the author. Afterwords are quite often used in books so that pertinent information will appear at the end of the literary work, and not confuse the reader.

This section will serve to give you other perspectives from some friends of mine who I truly respect. They were all handpicked for their perspectives because they are not only certified professionals in working with your kids; they care and are passionate about their work.

"You must keep an open mind. I try my hardest to stay unbiased as well. The majority of the youths that I deal with are extremely angry. They are drug users, gang members, prostitutes, child molesters, etc. Also, they're being raised either by their grandparents or by the system. The grandparents are afraid of their grandchildren. They don't have respect for authority because they didn't - or don't - have anyone to guide them on the right path and they don't hear the simple three words: "I Love You."

These youths aren't receptive towards you because of their disabilities. One common disability is illiteracy. This is very embarrassing for them. So instead of cooperating, they act out. They yell at you and become defiant. When it's time to go to school, they kick and scream or simply say, "I don't feel good." In all, nothing really can prepare you for this job, because every youth case is different. You don't know how they're going to react towards you. I just do the basics. I sit back and wait for him or her to calm down. Then, I'll ask if they're ready to talk. When they're ready, that's when I turn my full attention to them. Usually, I can get them to open up. They just have to trust that I'm not there to hurt them.

Approximately 12 years ago I had a minor who couldn't read and he wanted to learn. He wanted to write a letter to a judge. Well, I brought in a video called "You Can Read," along with the workbooks to help him. He asked me to help him when his peers weren't around. He was 16 years old and couldn't read. So, during recreation breaks, I'd work with him one-on-one. I also had him enrolled in Special Ed at the facility. By the time he was released, he was able to read at a fifth-grade level. He wrote his judge a letter, and also wrote me a "Thank You" letter for helping him. I ran across him years later in the mall, working at Mervyns. He told me that he got his GED and was enrolled in Junior College!

You have to listen to them. I've always been a very good listener and I take the time to listen to them. My parents always listened to my siblings and me. I guess that's where I got it. I really learn a lot from the youth, which helps me on a daily basis. I have to build up their confidence so they trust me. I need them to understand that I'm here to help them as best as I can, if they want the help. I'm not here to judge them. I require that they MUST respect me and most importantly themselves.

Afterword

I apply this to my life by ALWAYS talking to, not at, my daughters, and by listening to them. I tell them NOT to be a follower, be a leader. Keep GOD #1 in their lives and He'll continue to guide them in the right direction. I've taken my daughter to my job to show her what can happen if she decides to go on the wrong side of the road. I take the time to help my daughters with homework, support them in sports or whatever, make sure we tell each other I LOVE YOU, and most of all, pray."

- Shani Jackson, LA County Parole Officer, 16 years

"In my 19 years of teaching and coaching young people in high school, I have come to the realization that all kids want to feel valued. Whether teaching or coaching, I feel it's my duty to find something in them that they can feel proud of. Part of that duty is to make sure that I am consistent. If I say I am going to do something, I will do it. So many kids in the area I teach and coach do not have adults in their lives who they can rely on, look up to, or go to for support. For many kids, I am that person! That can be totally overwhelming at times, but I know if I am consistent and genuine they will get a sense of value and belief in themselves. That's really what it all comes down to: self-esteem. The kid who feels bad about himself, his home life, lack of parental support, etc., usually is not successful in the classroom. They really see no point to it . . . no value in who they are as people to know that they matter and that they can do great things.

On the other hand, these very same kids need a lot of structure! And that is also a consistency issue. The kids are very observant and if your structure - for example, your rules - are not the same for everybody or are not followed by you all the time, they will notice right away. My philosophy for teaching and coaching is one I borrowed from a mentor teacher in my first year teaching. This very simple motto has carried me through and is the backbone of my teaching/coaching style. It is the three "F"s: FIRM, FAIR and FLEXIBLE. This has helped me get through very tough decisions with students and athletes. The kids understand the three "F"s (provide structure) and also observe my consistency with them and their peers.

Being a track coach and running a team of 100+ athletes is a large undertaking. I would never take this job on or continue to do it even today without the great young people I get to work with daily. My team is actually one big diverse family. I used to be the auntie; but now that I'm older, I'm the mama! I have been included in their family celebrations, quinceañeras, weddings, funerals, birthday parties, college graduations . . . I know that I am a very important role model in their lives because of the care, consistency and value I show them. They mean a lot to me . . . and they mean a lot to each other.

One day, at the end of practice, a track parent rushed over to me as I was getting in my car to leave to tell me, "Robocop was shot." Robocop was the nickname of one of my hurdlers who had a very stiff style of running. I was stunned. I immediately asked where and if he was all right. The parent said that the ambulance was taking Robo to St. Francis in Lynwood. So I got in my car and drove as quickly as I could to the emergency room at St. Francis. The 15-minute ride was excruciating. I had no idea whether Robo was alive or dead or paralyzed. What was I going to tell the team, his mom, etc . . . How was I going to handle my own grief? I got into the

Afterword

emergency room and found many assistant coaches, parents, and team members already there. Everyone who heard the news came to give Robo and his family support and prayers. It was comforting to see the track family come together. It turned out that Robo got shot in the arm straight through, so he was going to be just fine. That experience proved to me that being a coach and a teacher is not a job at all. It is way deeper than that. It is a huge blessing and a huge responsibility."

- Chris Barboza, Teacher & Head Track Coach, 19 years Paramount High School

"What I have learned from the kids that I've dealt with is that we all go through struggles. Through life and growing up, school is one place where the kids are with us eight hours a day and their true personality, who they really are, normally comes out during that time. I have learned that it takes a lot of patience because everyone is coming from similar yet diverse backgrounds. Many kids need additional patience, additional counseling, additional time when it comes to getting through school, excelling in athletics, and just excelling in life (learning how to be bright young men and women). They also face having to be able to say no to certain life challenges, especially when they aren't beneficial to their well being.

When I speak of "challenges" I speak of things like gangs. Long Beach Polytechnic High School sits in the middle of a gang neighborhood, so the 20s, Insanes and other gangs are all around us. I know first-hand from growing up in this area, around 21st and Lewis, that the streets can consume you. A long time ago there was so much more respect for athletes. If the kid was not just going to school but was an athlete, there was somewhat of a respect; but now the gangs are approaching the players. Before there was enough respect to say, 'Not this one - not this kid,' or 'Let him go, he is on his way to practice.' There are days where I've had guys run up to me who didn't really know me, but somebody in the crowd would recognize me and say, 'That's the girl who runs track. Let her go, let her be.' They would leave me alone rather than attack me or feel me up or whatever. It's the same thing with the drugs. There was a lot more respect for the kids who were trying to do the right thing as opposed to others. The kids that were in church were labeled "church boy" or "church girl" and there was a level of respect. Those days are over. People don't seem to care about that anymore. I've had family members houses shot up with my grandmother standing right there. They didn't care.

My experience here teaches me how far I can or cannot take things when it comes to getting across to these kids. Some kids are dying for discipline and then some just don't have it. You can tell who doesn't come from a structured background. They are just looking for some structure to help guide them along their daily life. As someone who has grown up here, gone to school here, and lived here the majority of my life, I can relate more to some of the struggles they might be going through outside of school. When they come to school in the morning, they may not be in a great mood or they may be going through some stress. I don't take it personal. It isn't because of me as a teacher. Maybe they didn't get breakfast that morning. Maybe they didn't eat dinner that night. Maybe their parent is on drugs. Maybe their dad is an alcoholic, or their

Afterword

mom is an alcoholic. Maybe they're homeless or living out of a car.

It's up to me as a teacher to try and identify those kids - to know that it may not be just because they are poor. I have had kids that have been living out of a car for the majority of a school year. Homeless. I've had kids where the parents had cancer and were in the hospital, so they were left looking out for themselves. I've had kids whose parents would go to work before they got up in the morning, so it was up to them to wake themselves up and get to school everyday. Unfortunately, sometimes they don't get here; they're late or they miss every morning of my class. I recognize that this is a pattern. This is a problem. The parent is saying, "Well, I told them to get up" and they are just leaving it all in the kid's hands to raise themselves. The kids are saying, "I want someone to wake me up. I want someone to get me up in the morning. I want someone to help with homework and be there for me. I want someone to check on my grades. I want someone to talk to my teachers. I'm just out here doing whatever, and I would really like someone to be concerned about me. Even though they say they love me, it doesn't show in their actions."

You get to see so much through these kids' eyes, and if you talk to them, over time, when they learn to trust you, they start to share these things with you. It blows your mind. I just have to make sure we can get through day by day. I can't make plans for the next semester. They're in survival mode and just getting through.

Other kids have a great structure. They're doing well in school, everything they need is right there. It's not necessarily kids from a two-parent home. You can be in a single-parent home and get everything that you need. I was in a single-parent home and got what I needed. I also had coaches and other teachers, uncles and aunts, who were also making sure that I got whatever I needed and was looked out for. With the track team here at Poly having a 14-coach staff, we are coaches, we are counselors, we are second parents.

Sometimes things happen and it may not be what we SHOULD do, but sometimes those kids have to stay with you for a day or two because stuff is going on that is beyond their control. Or you have to find another parent who can be a surrogate parent for another family that needs help. Maybe they just don't have food tonight. You got to figure all that out.

Most people just see the finished product on the track or court or field, but it takes so much to get that athlete out there. There is so much that you're dealing with. There were not as many struggles in the 80s when I was in school, but now there are more people struggling than you can even imagine. And then there is just going through the struggle of being a teenager. Falling in love and trying to figure out . . . not just because someone says they love you, but because they really care about you, and they are going to love you regardless of whether you say yes or no to the pressure of being a teenager."

- Crystal Irving, Teacher & Girl's Athletic Director, 12 years Long Beach Polytechnic High School

Afterword

"Kids will come at you with what they know, what they've learned, and what works for them. Many times, we treat kids like the adults they are not. We expect things from them that they do not know, have not learned, or that are unfamiliar to their experiences.

I am an educator. I taught middle school and high school students for eight years and I now teach (train and coach) teachers on how to support student behavior at all grade levels. As an educator, I am still a student myself. I will never stop learning and my greatest, most profound teachers are the children and teens I work with.

To illustrate my point, I must tell you a little more about me, my path, and my passion for kids. As mentioned before, I taught middle school and high school students for several years. To be more specific, I taught a class specifically designed for students identified with "emotional or behavioral disorders." Now, I place that term in quotation marks because that is the state of California's designation of their challenges, not mine. My students were kids who lived in poverty, had fatherless homes (to reference an earlier section of Doc's book), experienced drug addiction of their own doing or a family member's, were involved in gangs, raised by grandparents and/or multiple foster homes, and often had less than stellar home environments. They were almost always Black boys. Now, let me be clear. I am a White female from an upper-middle-class upbringing, but I do not fit your typical "White girl" stereotype either (just ask Doc)! From my first day in the classroom, I instinctively knew I needed to get to know and understand these kids, their triumphs and their struggles, and the cultural/environmental differences from my own *childhood experiences. It was my responsibility, as their teacher, to teach from where "they were coming from" rather than from where I "expected" them to be.*

My first of many "A-ha" moments came during my first year in the classroom. One of my sixth-graders, Jamal*, was constantly falling asleep in class. Now, for any of you educators out there, you know that is a no-no! As a first-year teacher, I was especially sensitive to the idea of my principal walking in, seeing him sleeping, and it reflecting poorly on my teaching skills. Because of this, I tried everything I knew to keep him awake: begging, pleading, and threatening. And as you probably already guessed, none of it worked. I finally decided to make a contract with Jamal. This was the deal: if he could stay awake for at least ten days, I would take him out to lunch on a Saturday. Yes, I wanted him to stay awake and learn so badly that I was willing to give up my own free time to motivate and encourage him to do his part!

Well, after several weeks, he was able to meet his goal and we made plans (with his mother's permission, of course) to go to lunch the following Saturday. When I arrived at his apartment complex, I noticed three things: multiple complexes almost built on top of each other and that less than stellar (AKA "ghetto") neighborhood I mentioned earlier, and an older gentleman sitting on the stairs. As I approached his apartment, this older gentleman began catcalling various phrases and whistles that would make most women go off. Not knowing whom this man was, I ignored him. I knocked on Jamal's door and was greeted by his aunt, who yelled at Jamal, "Hurry up! Your teacher's here!" Jamal's aunt invited me in, to be polite I'm sure, and I was immediately taken aback by the cramped and overcrowded space.

To make a long story short, I asked Jamal about his living situation during lunch. He nonchalantly mentioned there were 13 people living in the two-bedroom apartment. His grandfather had one room, his mom and aunt shared a second, and all ten kids (five siblings and four cousins) fought for sleeping space on the living-room floor (not to mention the living room was small in and of itself). Now, I must tell you that Jamal, as a sixth-grader, was the oldest of the ten children. And I was worried about his sleeping in class? OK, maybe it was really more of a "DUH!" moment. No wonder he couldn't stay awake in class. He wasn't able to get a good night's sleep! He described having his siblings and cousins fighting for floor space, blankets, and pillows throughout the night. It had NOTHING to do with my teaching, my classroom, or me. How could I possibly fault this kid for falling asleep in class? Like a kick to the stomach, I was bombarded by the reality that Jamal was just trying to get by with the limited resources he had available. For Jamal, learning in school came second to getting food, sleep, and shelter on a consistent basis.

As my relationship with Jamal grew, I came to learn that the struggles he experienced on a daily basis had very little to do with an emotional or behavioral disturbance. He faced many of the struggles Doc discusses in his book. After my lesson learned, Jamal and I formed an agreement. When he was tired, he slept. Any work he missed, he would make up on his own time (and sometimes mine). But guess what? He did it! And all that "learning" I was afraid he would miss, he didn't. But his teacher was taught this important lesson: When a kid seems unmotivated, resistant, or even downright defiant, we can still make a difference by looking deeper into the situation and trying to understand where our kids are coming from. All kids deserve our patience, time, respect, and understanding, regardless of what they give (or don't give) us, because we're sometimes the only ones able to give it!"

- Stacie Alexander, MS, BICM
Educator & Behavior Specialist, 15 years
www.outsidethebox4kids.com

"shout out" scrapbook

You could just as easily ignore high school athletes or treat them as less important than Olympians . . . . but you don't. I appreciate so much that you treat me as though I am a superstar and that [you view] every single one of my races as Olympic trial quality. The moment I walked into your office, I felt a connection and comfort with every member of your staff that people don't usually feel in a doctor's office. Your attention to detail commands respect. Your kind demeanor calms me down (especially before races). Also, the personal responsibility you take helps every single athlete. Basically, you're awesome.

-Jaye Buchbinder, Chadwick School '11

I'd say that the last time you made me laugh is when you were telling me one of your stories. Your stories are hilarious! It was the one about the dude that fell asleep watching videos and woke up tucked in . . . LOL!!! As for the touching my life part, it's hard to say because almost every time I come to the office, you drop a lil encouragement on me in addition to fixing all the physical problems I come in with. Thank you Doc.

-Ronald Williams Jr, Long Beach City College Track & Field

"Shout Out" Scrapbook

Doc has been such an inspiration to me. He has touched my life in so many ways. He doesn't only nurse my injuries and help prevent them, he actually cares about his patients. Everyone that I have spoken to about Doc Dossman has been positive. He has mentored me on and off the field. After every race we analyze what I did and how we could both make it better. Doc Dossman is one of the most selfless human beings I have met. He is truly a beautiful person in my eyes and I love him with all my heart.

-Akawkaw Ndigpagbor, Future Olympian
2008 California State Champion/400m

Doc Dossman is an excellent doctor! He shows great pride in what he does. I like going to Doc because I feel a connection with him. He is always a phone call away! Thank you for being my doctor!

-Shalonda Solomon, USA Track & Field

Doc Dossman

I remember waiting in Doc's lobby and seeing this photo book with all kinds of pro and college athletes that he had worked with. I thought to myself, "Wow, this guy is famous." I had a pretty good relationship with Doc D. my freshman and sophomore year. Over the years we became a lot closer and I grew such a strong trust in him as he helped me come back from a serious injury. The summer of my sophomore year I broke my leg. I started physical therapy soon after I had surgery. However, as I was going through therapy, I felt that I was just another injured person showing up to someone's job. I wasn't getting much out of being there. When it came down to it, I knew I had to talk to Doc and see if he could help. I thought he probably might not have time or that I might not have the money to really get his help, but I showed up and it seemed like he was waiting for me! He came up with a rehab program for me and helped me get through the injury. The thing about it all is that we talked everyday that I came in. It wasn't just about the injury, but about school, family, anything that was on my mind. Through all the time I've spent with him I've gained so much respect and trust in his thoughts because they were never about irrelevant things. He always looked out for my best interest. Most importantly I'm sure that our friendship will never end. That's the best thing to me.

-Jamaal Grimes, Long Beach City College Baseball

"Shout Out" Scrapbook

Doc Dossman is the one person I trust when it comes to receiving treatment anytime, anywhere. He's the best! Doc has [a] great connection with the younger generation. It's great to have someone who is always welcoming and willing to be there to help, especially with athletes who are fully committed and serious. He's got humor, style, brains, and a heart sold out to Jesus. Doc Dossman is just an amazing person overall! He and his staff keep it real at the clinic. Every time I visit I always get the advice and treatment that I need. Thanks Doc for always being there!

-Krizia Leah Apelar, Cal State Fullerton Track & Field

Whenever I come into your office, you always say something that makes me laugh. Also, you don't just want our money. You take your time to get to know your patients as people. Every time I come to you with an injury, you get me back on the field ASAP... even if that means that weekend. You're like magic!!! Ok, I'm a fan! Doc, you have touched my life and inspired me to study Sports Medicine. When I grow up, I want to become the White Doc Dossman!!! :)

-Elliott Gentile,
Long Beach Poly Soccer

Since the day we met in '06, we clicked. You are the only person I can approach when I need to laugh, cry, gossip, or be put back in my place. You inspire and touch so many young people, me being one of them. I want to thank you for that. I love you Doc!

-Christina Harris,
"Your Favorite Daughter"

Throughout my sports career I have been blessed to be a patient of Doc Dossman and take advantage of his services. He has been instrumental to my success and for that I am grateful. He is also a great person to be around! I would like to thank him for the treatments. Much appreciated Doc!

-DeSean Jackson, WR, Philadelphia Eagles

"Shout Out" Scrapbook

Doc, you and I have become closer over the years. I trusted you with my body and ended up trusting you with more than that. Our connection is real and strong. I can call or text you anytime. I feel like we have grown through our prayers and everything has developed into what it is today. Thank you for all your support and believing in me when nobody else did. My 10th grade year I told you I was going to be #1 and I have been doing it ever since. It's been over 6 years and you have never let me down.

-Joey Hughes, 2008 California State Champion, 400m
USC Track & Field, 2010 Pac-10 Champion/400m

To say that he is my doctor wouldn't do the relationship I have built with him justice. He is my friend and confidant. He is someone I can talk to whenever I need. Doc is always there for me. He's a fun person to be around, but he makes sure he's someone in your life helping lead you in the right direction. He is always keeping me positive and focused on the important things in life. When you meet the Doc he welcomes you into his life with open arms, and you can't help but do the same. I've only known him for two years, but it seems like he's been in my life forever, there aren't many people that can make you feel that way, but Doc, well he's one of a kind.

-Rhyon Brown, Actress (Lincoln Heights- "Lizzie")

Thanks Doc for everything! You always get me back to 100% so fast and you've kept me healthy through the end of my high school career. I like to stick with who I know, so when I sign my NBA contract I want to be your first athlete to work you into his deal! Mark my word!!

-Demar Derozan, NBA Toronto Raptors

Doc isn't just my doctor; he is my brother. The trust I have in him is so deep that when I go to him I have no doubt in my mind that he WILL fix me. Years ago, I got hurt and Doc was the only one that knew what was wrong. He has always listened to me. He became the only doctor I trusted fully with my body. From track & field as a high school athlete to pregnancy, he has always been there. God put Doc in my life and I truly believe his hands are blessed. He is truly one of a kind and I love him very much.

-Nicole Duhart, UCLA graduate/New mother

Doc is the most real doctor I've ever been to. His work and the way he connects with his patients portrays the passion he has for helping heal his athletes. Whenever I came into his office, I had fun. Doc has a way of putting a smile on anyone's face. Although it's hard to have fun when you're injured, somehow Doc made it that way. When he fixed me up and sent me on my way, I was sad; sure I was healed, but that meant I didn't get to come into his office anymore! I trust him. I know he will be honest with me about both injuries and life in general. He's the best!!

-Jessica Brock, Long Beach Poly Soccer

Dossman is seriously the greatest. His office is always fun, and at the same time he always takes care of his patients. I know I can go to him for anything, and I really don't think I could've gotten through high school sports without his help. He cares about each of his patients so much and he builds relationships with each of us. I can talk to him about anything: sports, school, life. He really makes sure that he's more than a doctor, but a father figure to each of his patients as well. I'm so grateful to know Doc and I truly appreciate everything he has done for me.

-Megan Brock, Long Beach Poly Soccer

Doc Dossman

When we first met, I was depressed. I had just broken my knee cap and wasn't sure I was going to bounce back. You told me that you could help me. You said, "Come here everyday and we are going to get you back before your big tournament." It was so easy to talk to you because you listened first. You gave me advice and not so much of your opinion (never judging). I felt like I was your kid. Your hugs gave me the okay to come talk to you first when I needed help. You were never fake with me. You always kept it real. If I wasn't on my $h%t, you would tell me to step my game up. Most of all, you got my knee back on the right track. And if I say, "I'm hurting Doc," you would take care of that. You ma dog man! Nothing would ever change that. I love you.

-Brittany Brumfield, Trinity Valley JC
NJCAA Regional Champs

Thank you for always taking care of me when it is needed! Without you I probably would be working out in misery as well as pain. Thank you for always making treatments enjoyable with jokes, serious discussions, bright colored tape, and unforgettable stories! You have not just been an amazing doctor, but also a fantastic role model and a good friend.

-Erica Derrico, Your Favorite Pole Vaulter

Doc you already know what's up man! You have helped me on a lot! Especially them shins because they were killing me! I really appreciate what you have done for me. You are the BEST Doc ever, don't even trip! Thank you!

-Bryshon Nellum,
USC Track & Field
Gatorade National Boys Track & Field Athlete of the Year (2006-2007)

I like to call him "Dr. Trill Da Deal," because he the "Real Deal." Doc Dossman has never let me down. He has helped me on the high school level and the collegiate level. Now I plan on "going pro" and I look forward to using his services for the rest of my career!

-Stafon Johnson,
USC Trojans Football

Tennessee Titans (Rookie)

Doc Dossman

Doc Dossman never lets his age (as the adult) come between us (even though I am young). He listens respectfully to what I have to say. This makes it easier to trust him. It's like he understands every aspect of my situation or knows what to say when my problems don't seem to make sense. I look up to him as a father. He's my 2nd father. I can talk to him about those things I don't with my father. I love him and trust him with everything.

-Ashley Brown, "Your *Other* Favorite Daughter"

Thanks for all your hard work Doc! You have kept me on the field through high school and were still there for me while at Michigan. It doesn't stop here. Now I'm getting ready for the 2010 NFL Draft. See you at the top!

-Donovon Warren, CB
New York Jets (Rookie)

"Shout Out" Scrapbook

Doc Dossman has always been a father figure to me. He has talked me through many obstacles and given me excellent advice. Our relationship developed when I was in the 9th grade. He didn't make me feel young or try to tell me what to do with my life. He simply listened to what I had to say and gave advice when it was needed. We developed such a close relationship because I knew that I could trust him and that if I ever needed someone to lean on he would always be there for me. I realized I could trust Doc from the day we sat down and talked about the things I'd been going through. He saw the pain inside of me and instead of using my tribulations as a way to put me down, he uplifted me by letting me know that I was not alone. By attending Long Beach Polytechnic High School I have developed a village and I have gained many father figures and I am happy to say that Doc Dossman played an important role in my village. It takes a village to raise a child and I know this to be true from experience. Doc is a very positive role model to our community as a whole and I know that he will continue to touch many people in the future.

-Jasmine Joseph, 2007 California State Champion/400m
Cal Berkeley Track & Field

I remember meeting Doc and thinking, "This is gonna be an in-and-out thing." Little did I know, I was meeting a friend and a mentor. The reason so many young people connect with him is because for one: he's friggin' awesome!!! He shows mad respect and genuinely cares and wants to see his people succeed. Doc Dossman is truly the walking definition of "success."

-Jameia McDuffie, Hoop/Skater Girl

One of the things I appreciate about Doc Dossman is how down to earth he is. You walk in and sit down and he'll talk to you about his favorite new movie or crack a joke to ease any tension . . . and then he gets your needs taken care of. Fast. Visits to his office were so much fun that after I was better, I almost missed being injured.

-Oren Berkowitz,
Wise Beyond My Years

"Shout Out" Scrapbook

Doc Dossman is the man! He gets me back on the soccer field when I am injured. The guy knows what he is doing. I remember one time I was waiting for him in the treatment room. I started playing music from my iPhone. As soon as he walked into the room I shut it down and put it away. Doc smiles and says, "Go ahead man. Play your music. Show me what you got!" You should have seen his face when I pressed play. I don't remember what song it was, but it was Lil' Wayne!!

-Jack Davis, Long Beach Wilson Soccer

Before I met Doc, I hadn't met too many men I looked up to. He has given me hope that there are great men in this world. He has inspired me in so many ways. His guidance has helped me stay focused in school. Seeing what he has accomplished in his career makes me aspire to be more and accomplish more than he has. If not for Doc Dossman, I would be a typical student athlete with a typical major and the common attitude of many athletes who put their sport before their education. I am and will always be a better person because of that man, Dr. Craig Dossman, Jr.

-Courtney Clements, True Student-Athlete
San Diego State Women's Basketball

Doc, you have been the big brother and dad I always wanted growing up! You are very trustworthy and such a great people person. Our connection was instantaneous. We have a connection because we both have the will and drive to help and touch others throughout our lives. We are both leaders in our community and living out our God-given purpose. I am grateful for our connection. I love and trust you Doc.

-Taja Edwards, Fresno State Basketball

Doc Dossman is special because he is anointed of God. He not only heals the bodies of these kids, but he ministers to their minds. He cares and does not take his influence lightly. 'They become what they see', so it is very important that these kids see a young man like Doc out there on the sidelines. Many don't have any positive male role models in their lives, but Doc provides another option, and the kids identify with him. They love him.

-Coach Don Norford,
Long Beach Poly Track & Field

He has always been a great mentor as well as my friend. That relationship only enhanced our doctor/patient relationship. Things have only grown from there. Doc is like a father to me, but I love him like a brother.

-Isaiah Green, Fresno State Bulldogs Football

Thanks for all your support and all that you have done to help me. I wouldn't have been able to fix some of the problems I had without you. Thanks Doc, you are the best!

-Shana Woods, Heptathlete USC Track & Field

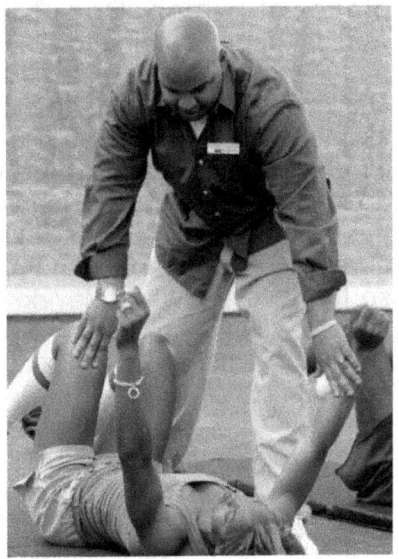

Doc and I met about 4 1/2 years ago. He has been my sports medicine doctor as well as a friend and role model. The thing that struck me most about Doc was he was a Black doctor, and not wearing a lab coat. The very look of him gave me hope that I too can persevere even though the color of my skin has kept so many of my kind down. The next thing that struck me was he was always willing and ready to listen to the kids. I cannot recall a time or place at which Doc wouldn't drop anything to help me through a challenge, whether it be track related or not. He was and is always there for me. He's like a big brother to me, so I trust him. He even prays with me whenever I ask. Sometimes I don't even have to ask. He just knows I need it. We call that the Holy Spirit. But over all I know Doc is just all for the kids; always. He's that non-judgmental outlet we all look for. He's so fun! We're always playing around in the office when I'm the last client of the day. Anyone who knows him loves his spirit and I believe it's his calling to mentor us. He's darn good at it.

-Turquoise Thompson
2009 California State Champion/400m
2010 Pac-10 Champion/400m Hurdles
UCLA Women's Track & Field

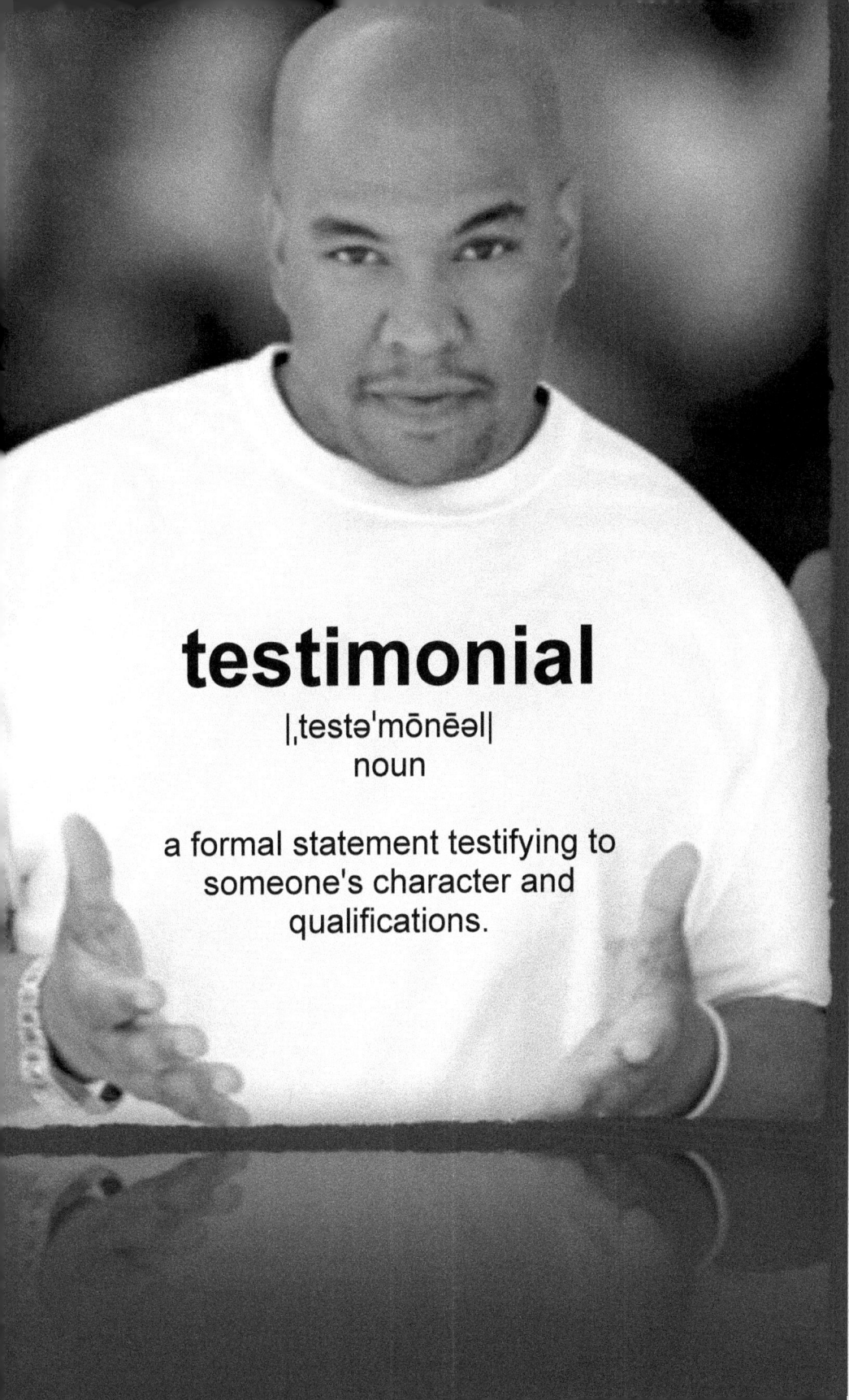

Phenomenal, awesome, professional, approachable! Doc Dossman is all of that! I have never met someone who is so passionate about their work, compassionate about their athletes/clients, professional in their field, yet approachable as a friend. I have coached on two International World Youth teams, for Italy, and Czech Republic, and I have yet to deal with any other doctor or trainer who has this combination.

-Lori Smith-Thompson
Head Manager IAAF USA World Youth Team 2009
Manager IAAF USA World Youth Team 2007
Head Coach, Gardena Serra Track & Field
Gardena, CA

Doc Dossman is special because he is anointed by God. He not only heals the bodies of these kids, but he ministers to their minds. He cares and does not take his influence lightly. "They become what they see," so it is very important that these kids see a young man like Doc Dossman out there on the sidelines. Many don't have any positive male role models in their life, but Doc Dossman provides another option, and the kids identify with him. They love him.

-Don Norford
Head Coach, Long Beach Poly High School Track & Field
Long Beach, CA

Doc saved me! He always comes through for me. He is a Godsend.

-Nicole Duhart
UCLA Women's Track & Field, Triple Jump

Doc Dossman

What you do for these kids and for the sport is so important. People really don't appreciate how necessary your services are in track and field. It is the only sport that requires you to push your body to the limit each and every single time you get on that line. In other sports you can rely on teammates and excel while playing injured. You can't play injured in track. It is the purest sport. In the olympics it is not called track and field, its called "athletics". You do a great service for the kids in our community and this program. You deserve to be saluted.

-Ron Alice
Head Coach, USC Track & Field

Reliable, hard-working, and passionate are the words that describe Doc Dossman. High school, college and world class athletes always gravitate back to him for his expertise. He is genuine.

-Jeanette Bolden
Head Coach, UCLA Women's Track & Field
Head Coach, U.S. Women's Olympic Team (Track & Field)
1984 Olympic Gold Medalist, 400m Relay

Thank you for taking the time out of your busy schedule to accompany me to Japan for the World Championships, to London, to the U.S. Olympic Trials, to Beijing for the Olympics, and everywhere else you go for me!

-Torri Edwards, Retired Olympian
2008 Olympic Finalist, 100m and 400m Relay
2007 U.S. Outdoor Champion, 100m
2007 World Outdoor Champion, 400m Relay
2003 World Outdoor Champion, 100m
2003 U.S. Outdoor Champion, 100m and 200m

Testimonials

I have known Doc Dossman for a few years now and he has helped my daughter in more ways than just her injuries. He helps build her confidence and determination to fight through the recovery stage. Doc always takes the time to show he cares. These young athletes need top rate medical treatment, but also need to know they are important as athletes and to know that the doctor treating them really cares about their success. We always get this with Doc. I will never forget our first experience. My daughter, Adriana Santillan, walked in on crutches, and walked out holding her crutches in her hand and laughing because she couldn't believe how good her ankle felt. Thank you Doc for all of the love you put into what you do. Thank you for what you have done for my daughter and for all of our young soccer players at FC Long Beach!

-Fabian Santillan
President & Coach, FC Long Beach Soccer Club
Head Girls Varsity Soccer Coach, St. Anthony High School
Long Beach, CA

Doc, I want you to know that I appreciate you always coming through for me. Making the U.S. team is not just a win for me but for you as well. You are just as much a part of this as me and my coach. I don't want you to think that all your hard work on me has gone unnoticed. Thank you.

-Shawn Crawford, Nike Track & Field
4x U.S. Outdoor Champion ('01, '02, '04, '09), 200m
2008 Olympic Silver Medalist, 200m
2004 Olympic Gold Medalist, 200m
2004 Olympic Silver Medalist, 400m relay

I am very confident in the work that Doc Dossman does for me. He has kept my body healthy and ready to run for a very long season. Since I've been working with him I'm very confident that I will not have any repeat hamstring issues.

-Carmelita Jeter, Fastest Woman Alive
2010 World Indoor Championships Bronze Medalist, 60m
2010 U.S. Indoor Champion, 60m
2009 U.S. Outdoor Champion, 100m
2x World Outdoor Championships Bronze Medalist, 100m

Throughout my sports career I've been blessed to be a patient of Doc Dossman and take advantage of his services. He has been instrumental to my success and for that I am grateful.

-DeSean Jackson
Philadelphia Eagles NFL Wide Receiver, #10
2009 All-Pro as Punt Returner
Cal Bears Football (2005-2007)
3x All-American as Punt Returner and Wide Receiver
2x All-Pac-10 as Punt Returner and Wide Receiver
Long Beach Poly High School Class of 2005
Parade Magazine High School All-American
2005 MVP of the U.S. Army All-American Bowl
2004 Long Beach Poly's CIF-SS Championship Team Member
2004 Mr. Football State Player of the Year
(Patient since 2003)

Testimonials

Doc Dossman is not only invaluable for his services to our athletic department, but for his role as a mentor to so many of our kids.

-Rob Shock
Athletic Director, Long Beach Poly High School
Long Beach, CA

I have worked with Doc Dossman on a medical response team since 2004. We work the National Scholastic Indoor Championships in NYC every year. He is very quick on his feet, confident, competent, and a pleasure to work with! I trust him completely.

-Troy Lee
Paramedic/EMT
New York City, NY

Doc, I want to thank you for the help healing my hamstring when I was in desperate need [while in high school]. It was much appreciated!

-O.J. Mayo
Memphis Grizzlies NBA, #32
NBA All-Rookie First Team
USC Trojans Basketball
2008 All-Pac-10 Player
3x State Basketball Champions (Huntington High School),
Huntington, West Virginia
EA Sports Nat'l High School Boys Basketball Player of the Year
McDonald's All-American
3x Parade All-American
2x Ohio's Mr. Basketball

Hey Doc, I just want to thank you for the work on my shoulder. I was dying out there everyday in summer workouts trying to get that crucial upper body work in before the season and the treatments really knocked out my shoulder pain. I appreciate it! Without you, I just might be two steps behind out there on the turf!

-Terrence Austin
2010 NFL Rookie (Washington Redskins)
Former UCLA Football Wide Receiver & Kick Returner, #4
Lettered 4 years at Long Beach Poly (Football/Track)
National Scholastic Indoor Pentathlon Champion
U.S. Army All-American Game Participant
(Patient since 2003)

When someone cares it is manifested by their actions and deeds. Doc Dossman is visible . . . and goes above and beyond for our young people.

-Coach Robert King
Co-Founder Quiet Fire Youth Track Club
Assistant Track & Field Coach, St. Mary's Academy
Inglewood, CA

I'm a 53-year-old female marathon runner. I've been receiving treatment from Doc for the past few years. Thanks to Doc, his sports medicine expertise, and breakthrough taping techniques, I've been able to continue to enjoy my passion for running!

-Danna Duncan
Marathoner

Testimonials

I've worked with a bench of physical therapists, chiropractors, massage therapists and trainers in Europe, but Doc Dossman showed me another way to heal and most of all understands my body and its own language. [As] an athlete there is nothing more important than mastering the body and he helped me do that. He followed me every session (never looking his watch) in order to set me free from EVERYTHING that can impede me to run with a free mind.

-Martial Mbandjock, Mizuno Track & Field
2008 French National Champion, 100m
2009 French National Champion, 200m
2009 World Championships Semi-Finalist 200m
2008 Olympics Semi-Finalist, 100m
2008 World Indoor Championship Semi-Finalist, 100m

I call Doc "The Professional Good Day Haver." He has a smile and a wholesome outlook everyday. I appreciate his service because of the fun atmosphere he invokes and knowledge he brings. He seeks to resolve the source of the injury, not just treat the pain. That's why I like him. His innovative ways mixed with traditional knowledge keep him progressive and current in modern solutions. He works for solutions and prevention!

-Darrell Smith
World-Class Professional Track Coach (DSports)

Doc Dossman is the rare occurrence of a highly skilled professional with charisma and knowledge of today's pop culture. It's like having your close friend as your doctor.

-Bashir Ramzy
USA Track & Field Long Jumper

Doc Dossman

I have been working with Doc Dossman for over two years now, and within those two years as a patient he has helped me to stay healthy and injury-free throughout my seasons.

-Andrea Bliss, Puma International
Jamaica Track & Field, Hurdles

Doc Dossman has been treating me for the last 5 years. His treatments and techniques have allowed me to continue to be able to play the game I love. Without a doubt, Doc Dossman has added longevity to me as a coach and teacher at Long Beach Poly. Of course I appreciate what he does for my boys. Doc is the name that comes to mind when I see one of my kids go down with an injury.

-Sharrief Metoyer, Head Boys Basketball Coach
Long Beach Poly High School
Long Beach, CA

I came to see Doc Dossman on a recommendation of my teammate, and I had a great experience. His knowledge and skill aided me when I strained my piriformis and got me healthy to be able to compete through it. I love how Doc Dossman is passionate about helping and his skills are hard to beat. His services are valuable and his friendship is invaluable.

-Logan Taylor
Former USC Track & Field Athlete, 110m Hurdles
Assistant Track & Field Coach, El Camino College
Compton, CA

Testimonials

Doc Dossman is a one of a kind. He is diligent in his chosen field of sports medicine as well as in the lives of the young athletes he treats. He listens, relates, encourages and inspires these young athletes to not only do well in their athletic endeavors but to become the best people they can become through character and compassion. As an educator and coach, he serves as a real support in what I am trying to accomplish with these young, talented kids.

-Christine Barboza
English/Language Arts Teacher
Head Track & Field Coach, Paramount High School
Paramount, CA

You could just as easily ignore high school athletes or treat them as less important than Olympians . . . but you don't. I appreciate so much that you treat me as though I am a superstar and that [you view] every single one of my races as Olympic trial quality.

-Jaye Buchbinder
Middle Distance Runner, Chadwick School Class of 2011,
Palos Verdes Peninsula, CA

On behalf of the Lady Jackrabbits and our coaching staff, I'd like to thank Doc Dossman for his time and invaluable contributions to maintaining the health and fitness of our team. We look forward to a continued relationship with you as we fight for our third straight California State Championship.

-Carl Buggs, Head Girls Basketball Coach
Long Beach Poly High School
Long Beach, CA

Doc Dossman

Doc is committed and selfless. He will go the extra mile to figure out what's wrong with you and help you get better. Thanks for being my "Go-to-Guy" Doc!

-Rhonda Watkins
UCLA Women's Track & Field, Long Jump/High Jump
2008 Trinidad and Tobago Olympian, Long Jump
2007 NCAA Indoor and Outdoor Champion, Long Jump
2006 World Junior Champion, Long Jump

Doc you already know what's up, man! You helped me on a lot! Especially them damn shins because they where killing me! I really appreciate what you have done for me. You are the BEST Doc ever. Don't even trip! Thank you!

-Bryshon Nellum
USC Track & Field
2007 Gatorade National Boys Track & Field Athlete of the Year
2007 Pan Am Junior Athletic Championships: Gold Medalist (400m) & Silver Medalist (1600m Relay)
2005 USA Youth Outdoor Track & Field Champion, 200m
2x California State Champion, 200m
2x California State Champion, 400m
California State Champion, 400m & 1600m relays
National Record Holder, 800m Sprint Medley Relay
Long Beach Poly High School Track & Field
(Patient since 2003)

Doc Dossman is the REAL DEAL! I appreciate what you did for me man.

-Thomas Howard
Mr. 53, Oakland Raiders NFL Linebacker

Testimonials

It's a guarantee that Doc Dossman will find anything and everything wrong with your body and heal it! He is the best in his field.

-Ginnie Crawford, History in the Making!
2010 U.S. Indoor Champion, 60m Hurdles
2x U.S. Outdoor Champion, 100m Hurdles ('06 & '07)
2x NCAA Outdoor Champion, 100m Hurdles ('05 & '06)

Working with Doc Dossman was an excellent experience! I injured my hamstring at the U.S. National Championships. After seeing Doc several times in that single weekend, I noticed a dramatic improvement in my hamstring. The soreness and inflammation decreased immensely and he was very informative on every treatment he did. I like to call him the "Gentle Giant." Thanks for everything Doc! I always look forward to working with you.

-Me'Lisa Barber
2006 World Indoor and U.S. Indoor Champion, 60m
2006 Indoor VISA Championship Winner
2005 U.S. Outdoor Champion, 100m
2005 World Outdoor Champion, 400m Relay

Doc Dossman is the reason I can still play at this level today. He has helped me through some serious injuries. He not only healed my body but he has also given me hope. He is like a big brother to me. I know that I can count on him no matter what any other doctors may tell me. Thanks for everything Doc!

-Chauncey Washington
New York Jets NFL Tailback, #32
Former USC Football Tailback, #23

Doc Dossman

Doc Dossman is one of the best. He is young and doing his thing! Whenever something is hurting me, he is the man I go see. Thanks for everything Doc!!!

-Davon Jefferson
Former USC Trojans Basketball, #5

Doc has been with me since my freshman year in high school. He is the best! My knees feel brand new after my cold laser treatments!

-Jasmine Dixon
UCLA Women's Basketball, #33
2008 McDonald's All-American
2008 Gatorade California Player of the Year
2008 L.A. Times Player of the Year
3 California State Titles, Long Beach Poly High School
Named 1st Team All-American by Parade Magazine, USA Today, EA Sports, and ESPN HoopGurlz

Doc Dossman is an excellent doctor! He shows great pride in what he does. I like going to Doc Dossman because I feel a connection with him. He is always there when I have a problem or he is always a phone call away! Thank you for being my doctor!

-Shalonda Solomon
University Of South Carolina Track & Field Sprinter
2007 SEC Outdoor Champion, 200m
2006 NCAA Indoor Champion, 200m
2006 NCAA Champion, 200m
2005 NCAA Indoor National Champion, 1600m Relay
2x Gatorade National Female Athlete of the Year ('03 & '04)
10x All-American
8x Record-Setting Relay Team Anchor, Long Beach Poly

Testimonials

He has not only an understanding of how the body works and moves, but Doc also appreciates that even though we are all of similar build, there is not just one way to treat us. This is very rare! He hasn't let me down yet!! Thanks Doc!!

-Felix Sanchez, Dominican Republic Track & Field
3x World Champion, 400m Hurdles ('01, '03 & '07)
2004 Olympic Gold Medalist, 400m Hurdles

Thanks for all your support and all that you have done to help me. I wouldn't have been able to fix some of the problems I had without you. Thanks Doc, you are the best!

-Shana Woods
USC Track & Field, Heptathalon, Long Jump & Relays
High School All-American
Member of National Indoor Record Setting Teams:
800m Relay & 400m Relay, Long Beach Poly
2006 USA Track & Field Jr. Heptathlon Champion
National High School Record Holder in Heptathlon
(First high school girl to ever score over 5,500 points)
2005 U.S. Team for the Youth Championships in Morocco
2004 California State Long Jump Champion

Meeting Doc Dossman and experiencing his cold laser technology was one of the best things that I could have done for my professional career. His professionalism and knowledge for the athletic body makes him one of the finest doctors in Southern California.

-Marques Anderson
Retired Oakland Raiders NFL Strong Safety, #34

Doc Dossman

I really love coming to Doc's office because he takes such good care of my body. Doc is very knowledgeable and has taught me so much. He is someone I can trust. He is more than my doctor, he is my friend!

–Nichole Denby, Nike Track & Field
2005 U.S. Nationals Finalist
2004 U.S. Olympic Trials Finalist
7x Track & Field All-American
3x Track & Field Big 12 Conference Champion

I know that if I am injured I can trust that Doc will take care of me and he will see to it that I can get back on the track as fast as possible. He is definitely my favorite doctor. Thanks Doc Dossman for all you have done for me.

-Ebony Collins, Nike Track & Field
2005 USA Track & Field Youth Athlete of the Year
2005 IAAF World Junior Champion Silver Medalist (100m) & Gold Medalist (400m Hurdles)
3x USA Track & Field Junior Olympics Gold Medalist, 400m Hurdles ('04, '05, '06)
3x USA Track & Field Youth Outdoor Champion Gold Medalist, 400m Hurdles ('03, '04, '05)

Just wanted to say thank you . . . You really helped me recover fast and got me where I needed to be for my pro day. Thanks Doc!

-Manuel Wright
Stockton Lightening (Arena Football)
Former USC Football Defensive Tackle, #92

Testimonials

Doc Dossman's chiropractic and massage treatments have taken my athletic performance to another level. The background of my success is contributed to his expertise and desire to make my career excel at maximum levels. [Doc], I can thank you for helping me become a World Champion for the fifth time.

-Tyree Washington
World Class 400-meter Specialist
2006 Olympic Gold Medalist, 1600m Relay

Your medical tactics and knowledge helped me stay on the court at times any other doctor would have told me to rest. As a result, I walked away my senior year with a state championship ring. Continue to do what you do for the athletes who, like me, appreciate it.

-April Phillips
Xavier Women's Basketball #42
2x Nike All-American
Professional Women's Basketball, Poland

Doc is one of the best docs around. He not only defeats the impossible, but restores the truth!

-Taja Edwards
Fresno State Women's Basketball #1
3x WAC Conference Champions
3x WAC Tournament Champions
2x CIF Champions (Long Beach Poly Girls Basketball),
Back-to-Back State Champions
McDonald's All-American Candidate

Doc "BOSS-MAN" has been one of the most positive people in my life. He has helped me with my injuries and much more. He always has open ears willing to listen and learn. The whole office is flat out the BEST to work with. With "BOSS-MAN" and family you will never go wrong. Much love always!

-Isaiah Green
Fresno State Bulldogs Football Cornerback, #10
2005 World Youth Games Champion, Sprint Medley Relay
2004 USA Track & Field Junior Olympics Silver Medalist

After working with Doc Dossman, I noticed more flexibility, reduced swelling, minimal pain in both knees, and an immediate change in my posture. He has helped me with [everything from] back spasms, to posture, to rehabbing two knee surgeries. I feel at home in his work environment and appreciate all his services. He has been and still is an excellent help and friend to my family and to me.

-Chanda Picott
UC Berkeley Track & Field Sprinter

My treatment at Doc's office has helped me improve my technique and has made me better in a number of events. The treatments have also helped me to stay healthy so that I can be at my best during my season.

-Jaime Allen-Cuthbert, Heptathlete
Cal State University Long Beach Women's Track & Field
Long Beach, CA

Testimonials

Thanks for all the support and treatments! I feel much better knowing that you are there!

-Travon Patterson
USC Trojans Football Wide Receiver, #17
USC Trojans Track & Field Sprinter

The treatment I receive at Doc's office keeps me able to play at the best of my abilities without worrying about any injuries. Any little nagging pains I feel can be treated with a new technology that Doc Dossman uses called the cold laser. It takes any nagging pains away instantly!

-Darnell Bing
Houston Texans NFL Linebacker, #50
USC Trojans Football Co-Captain & Strong Safety, #20
2005 All-American
2004 & 2005 National Champs

I first connected with Doc Dossman going into the 2007 NFL draft out of the University of Washington. When I say he couldn't [have] come at a better time, I mean it! I had suffered a high-ankle sprain that limited a lot of things for me, such as: range of motion, flexibility, and lower-body strength. After a few sessions I felt a dramatic change in my mobility and strength-gain. This guy is educated and takes his job seriously, especially when it comes to [treating] athletes because he knows what our bodies go through on a day-to-day basis. GO Dossman!

-Dashon Goldson
San Francisco 49ers NFL Safety, #38

Doc Dossman

Doc is such a special man! I truly believe that he was sent by God to help others. It's amazing to me how much he cares to help other athletes reach their goals. He has one of the biggest hearts I have ever seen. So, if nobody ever says it, "THANKS 4 everything Doc." I'm not done. If Doc wasn't sent to me at the right time, I really was close to giving up on track. Our pep talks and his daily words of encouragement kept me going. There were times when I didn't think that I would amount to anything. Going to college was something I didn't think I could do. Knowing how bad things got my senior year (with injuries) and not being able to put some times down, I didn't believe I was going to get a scholarship. I knew my parents weren't going to help me. I felt like I could talk to Doc about anything - from problems at home to school issues, and even on spiritual things. There are people like Doc, who on a daily basis I think about when times get hard (practice). . . I can't let them down, and more importantly I can't let myself down. So once again I say, "Thank you. Love you much Doc! Straight From the Heart!"

-Shana Solomon
San Diego State University Women's Track & Field
2007 NCAA Championships Qualifier, 100m & 200m
2007 USTFCCCA All-West Region Honors:
100m, 200m, & 400m Relay
Member of National Indoor Record Setting Teams:
800m Relay & 400m Relay, Long Beach Poly

I would have never been healthy enough to compete for my scholarship to UCLA if it weren't for Doc Dossman!!

-Justin Brown
UCLA Bruins Football Offensive Tackle, #76

Testimonials

Before I met Doc Dossman, I injured my hamstring seven times while running track. I've struggled with hamstring injuries since I was a sophomore in high school. I met him as a Junior attending USC . . . I was sure this would just be another sports medicine appointment that would just give me maintenance. No . . . Doc Dossman gave me causation, prevention, fixation, and hope. If Doc told me I could run full out at 100% and I felt a soreness in my leg, without a shadow of a doubt I knew I could go out there and run at 100% and not reinjure my leg. That was indeed a first. Up until this day I will continue to make my appointments with him and make referrals to other elite athletes. Thank you Doc Dossman!

-Nia Ali
USC Track & Field Heptathlete and Hurdler
2009 Second All-Time Best Heptathalon for a USC Female
2008 Fourth All-Time Best 100m Hurdles for a USC Female
2008 SEC Heptathalon Champion as a Freshman at the University of Tennessee
2007 SEC Outdoor Track & Field Freshman Runner of the Year

I went to his office to have work done on my lower back which was giving me a great deal of problems. Doc Dossman was able to instantly give me relief. I thank him for that because he was a tremendous help.

-Rodney Van
UCLA Bruins Football Cornerback, #3
Former San Jose Sabercats (Arena Football)
Hamilton Tiger Cats (Canadian Football League), #8

Doc Dossman

Doc is the best around. With his muscle strengthening and cold laser treatments, I was able to fully recover from ankle surgery. A family member recommended Doc and I've been going back ever since. The services are excellent and I would recommend Doc to all student-athletes and professionals across the country. You will be pleased with the results.

-Marcus Everett
Former UCLA Bruins Football Wide Receiver, #9
Milwaukee Iron, Arena Football League, #8

I would like to take this time to express my extreme appreciation for all of your help these past few years. You have been great in my preparation for the 110 meter high hurdles as a Masters athlete. You have educated me in the areas of sports injury and rehabilitation that has allowed me to continue to compete at a high level. As a high school sprint and hurdle coach at Roosevelt high school in Corona, you have been an integral part of our team's success as we have one of the top teams in California. My athletes enjoy coming to see as they know they will be physically improved when they leave your office. They also enjoy your open and warm personality as you are able to relate to them in such a positive manner. I [continue to] look forward to working with you as a coach and athlete. We feel very fortunate to have you as part of our team as you are a valuable asset to our program.

-Henry Andrade
Assistant Track Coach, Roosevelt High School
Corona, CA

Testimonials

I have had the pleasure of working with Doc Dossman for two years and it has been an absolute pleasure. Doc Dossman has kept me in one piece and is still keeping me in one piece today. Thank you for all your help thus far and I look forward to working with you in 2012 (London Olympics). Let's bring home the GOLD!!!

-Tyrone Edgar, Great Britain Track & Field
2009 World Championship Bronze Medalist, 400m Relay
2008 Olympic Semi-Finalist, 100m

I used to get serious injuries and not be able to train at 100% every season . . . but since working with Doc Dossman I'm almost injury-free so I'm able to train hard without being worried about my body. I can be focused on running fast instead of thinking about not hurting myself because Doc Dossman keeps me in the greatest shape I had ever been before. He always has the right solution and the problem doesn't last. [I call him] Doc "King of Therapists" Dossman!

-Teddy Venel, France Track & Field
2008 Olympic Qualifier, 1600m Relay

The techniques used to treat me were great and [your staff] was great as well. I now recommend Doc Dossman to all of the athletes I know!

-Larry Croom
Pittsburgh Steelers NFL Running Back, #30
Former UNLV Running Back, #1

Doc Dossman

I've been in martial arts/Brazilian Jiujitsu as well as being a strength and conditioning coach for many years. With all of the athletes and clients I have had and my personal experience with injuries, there has never been a doctor that was worked as well with his clients and as effectively with his clients as Doc. His ground-breaking methods have changed the course of my athletic career. I have the privilege of being his jiujitsu instructor, and his knowledge of the human body and how it works with the mind gives him a unique insight as a martial arts student.

-Preston Rawlings
Brazilian Jiujitsu Instructor
Strength and Conditioning Coach
Lakewood, CA

Doc Dossman has perfected his ability to heal and inspire those he comes in contact with. His love of sports provides a caring approach to an athlete's preparation and/or return to competition. He has a great knack for maintaining a professional presence in an athlete's life as well as infusing humor and an overall feeling of positivity. He is a great role model of health and fitness himself. I know if I have an athlete that needs to return to action, Doc Dossman is the MAN! The girls on the Long Beach Poly Girls Soccer team refer to his practice as the "Dossman Magic."

-Teri Collins
Physical Educator
Head Girls Varsity Soccer Coach, Long Beach Poly High
Long Beach, CA

Testimonials

I know Doc as both a client and a friend. As someone I entrust to help get me ready to compete to the best of my ability, he has been instrumental in giving me the best treatment possible and introducing me to his cutting edge taping techniques, DAT. He is also one of the most positive, upbeat people I know, with an enthusiasm for his career and life in general that is unmatched. Surrounding myself with people like Doc has not only made me a better athlete, but a better person as well.

-Brianna Glenn, USA Track & Field
2009 U.S. Outdoor Runner-Up, Long Jump
2002 U.S. Outdoor Champion, Long Jump
2002 NACAC Long Jump and 400m Gold Medalist
2001 NCAA 200m & Long Jump Champion
2x Pac-10 Athlete of the Year ('00 & '01)

I have benefited in so many ways from utilizing Doc Dossman's expertise. He is a valuable asset to our sports medicine team at Long Beach Poly. His input has taken our athletes to another level. He exposes our athletes to things that athletes usually don't see until they are a high collegiate or professional athlete.

-Davion White, MA, ATC
Head Athletic Trainer, Long Beach Poly High School
Long Beach, CA

Nobody got hands like Doc! Nobody!

-Lester Speight, aka Mighty Rasta,
aka Reebok's Terry Tate, Office Linebacker

Doc Dossman

Doc Dossman is one of the best sport therapists around. I have had the pleasure of working with him since 2005 until now. He has the ability to make anyone feel comfortable and puts optimal effort in making sure his clients are healthy. His great commitment to the community and helping high school students excel is undeniable. He is a helping hand in these kids' lives and can relate to them on many different levels. His unconventional ways in the office attract a diverse crowd and plenty of young adults. With his youthfulness, laid back demeanor, casual dress, love for music and magical hands, Doc Dossman is a humanitarian, and inspiration to everyone.

-Miki Barber
2007 U.S. Outdoor Championship Finalist, 100m and 200m
2001 World Championship Semi-Finalist, 1600m Relay
2000 U.S. Olympian, 1600m
1999 World University Games Champion, 1600m Relay
16x All-American
11x SEC Champion
4x NCAA Champion

I like to call him "Doc Trill Da Deal," because he the "Real Deal." Doc Dossman has never let me down. He has helped me on the high school level and now on the collegiate level. I plan to "go pro" someday and I look forward to using his services for the rest of my career!

-Stafon Johnson
2010 NFL Rookie (Tennessee Titans)
Former USC Trojans Football Running Back, #13

Testimonials

It would be easy to say about Doc Dossman all of the phrases one typically repeats about a competent healthcare provider. He is the consummate professional – caring, personable, and knowledgeable. He is open to and seeks input from coaches and parents. And, I realized the very first time I sent an athlete to see him, that his understanding of the doctor-patient relationship was different. I expected this young lady to return from her first appointment with "Doc" with a new understanding of what might be causing her aches and pains. But, I was surprised at how excited she seemed because she now carried within her a completely new understanding of her personal role and responsibility for maintaining her own health. Moreover, she wasn't told she had to "take time off" or "back off." Rather, she was provided tools and knowledge that helped her to enhance her performance. It wasn't long before more and more athletes began making the trek to his office. By connecting with each athlete on a personal level, Doc Dossman takes the "therapeutic relationship" to a new level – a level where healing the soul is as crucial as healing the body.

-Ralph P. Casas, Pharm.D., Ph.D.
Head Cross Country/Track & Field Coach,
La Mirada High School, CA
Professor, Health Occupations, Cerritos College, CA

I came to know this young doctor through my sons. My son Isaiah Green, of Long Beach Poly High School, lived to run and was deemed by the high school sports world to be one of the best sprinters in the state of California.

Unfortunately, he was injured two years in a row which not only took a toll on his body, but for his young mind it was devastating. He felt life had given up on him. I was a single mom with two high school boys and knew little about sports injuries and how to help my son recover. My insurance would not cover his athletic needs and with the same urgency. Doc saved my son's life. Not only did he immediately treat his injuries, but he became a friend and father figure to Isaiah which gave him hope to continue dreaming, living and striving for excellence. Isaiah is currently a junior in college at California State University, Fresno on a football scholarship. He [Doc] became the doctor of choice among young people, someone who they could trust, respect, and someone who was willing to listen and in most cases be able to help. It is so important that our young people have young intelligent, safe and respectful adults that they can turn to and trust. This is a young man who has been a giver and supporter of our young community. He should be acknowledged and celebrated for his endless giving. He is a responsible teacher of valuable and useful content. He is set apart from the rest. He offers to his young patient's information, education, inspiration, motivation and hope! Doc Dossman literally is saving lives, he his able to build positive relationships with students, coaches and parents that supports a positive community in which these students can draw from.

-Alice Green
Mother of Isaiah Green,
Fresno State Bulldogs Football, Cornerback, #10
2005 World Youth Games Champion, Sprint Medley Relay
2004 USA Track & Field Junior Olympics Silver Medalist

Testimonials

Doc Dossman, you are amazing! I appreciate your expertise and genuine concern for our athletes. You not only prepare them for competition, you include life lessons while you're treating them. My daughter looks forward to coming into your office. Your personality is inviting and she feels comfortable with you. The office staff is a reflection of you as well. Without you, I don't know how she could continue to run at her desired level. You are sympathetic to her but you also know when to tell her to just "man up" and get it done. I am so relieved sometimes when I can get her to you because you often reassure me that her aches and pains are normal. I would highly recommend your services to any athlete, no matter their level of competition. You Are The Best! Thank you for all that you do . . .

-Michelle Wilson
Mother of Brianna Wilson,
Los Osos High School Track & Field Sprinter
Rancho Cucamonga, CA

My daughter is an elite athlete from Philadelphia, Pennsylvania, who has struggled with hamstring injuries. When she decided to attend USC in Los Angeles, California, I suffered from anxiety because she would be so far away from home without the physical therapist that had been working with her throughout high school. Another USC athlete referred us to Doc Dossman and from her first visit, I felt at ease. He has a complete understanding of each athlete's body and from the beginning I knew I could trust what he said. Upon treating my daughter, he let her know that it was okay to take her body to the limit without fear of that hamstring being an issue. Doc Dossman's constant pursuit of new and innovative methods of treatment lets me know that my daughter is in the perfect position to excel without fear. We will continue to count on his expertise!

-Melita Johnson
USC Track & Field Heptathlete and Hurdler
2009 Second All-Time Best Heptathalon for a USC Female
2008 Fourth All-Time Best 100m Hurdles for a USC Female
2008 SEC Heptathalon Champion as a Freshman at the University of Tennessee
2007 SEC Outdoor Track & Field Freshman Runner of the Year

Doc, you have been such a blessing to our family, especially to Tamarah. It's been over a year since she began treatments with you and you've made all the difference in her game. You've kept her on the field. Amazingly, I didn't realize how much constant pain she was experiencing, but you've given her such relief. The smile that comes over her face as you approach her with that bear hug, just before the snap, crackle, pop is a pleasure for me to witness. I also love the influence you have with her. She loves sharing all the unnecessary, yet so necessary, details of her life . . . simply because she believes you care and actually listen. And I know it isn't just her, because I see the transformation that takes place with other patients. They may walk in quiet and solemn, but they leave with energy and enthusiasm . . . from the oldest to the youngest. You are a people person. You keep it real. You speak the language of the youth to the youth. You engage the concerns of the parents without sugar coating. You're worth the hour-and-a-half [drive] on

Testimonials

the return back to the Inland Empire. Yeah, you're pretty special to us and we wouldn't trade you for anything.

-Alva Stewart
Mother of Tamarah Stewart,
Premier Club Soccer Player
Rancho Cucamonga, CA

Doc Dossman has been a great doctor but also a good friend to my daughter and me. When I visit his office I feel like I am at home because of the music, the interaction between the staff, and most of all, Doc's stories. He is an excellent doctor and he takes pride in his practice and his patients. When we enter his office we know we will come out healed! Keep using those healing hands. Thanks for being who you are Doc and God bless you.

-Rita Reels
Mother of Melia Cox,
Long Beach Poly High School Track & Field
Long Beach, CA

Doc Dossman began treating my son Devan just over a year ago. Besides healing his body, Doc has helped to prepare a young man for college both mentally and physically. With his welcoming smile, he makes you feel more like a family member or a long time friend instead of just a patient. I feel blessed to have had someone care for and treat my son as if he was his own. Doc, you are more than a doctor, you are also a mentor and a friend!

-Bridgette Thomas
Mother of Devan Spann,
Arizona State Sun Devils Football, Cornerback
Gardena, CA

Doc Dossman

Doc Dossman is the greatest . . . he is always there for our kids and sometimes for the parents too! Doc is a person that takes his profession to heart and he puts everything into it - mind, wisdom, experience, and of course God - when working on our kids. He keeps the kids in good health and makes sure they are capable of running. We are getting ready for state . . . see you there Doc!

-Sylvia Reed-Lyday
Mother of Carisma Lyday,
Long Beach Poly High School Track & Field
Long Beach, CA

Doc Dossman has been very influential to my daughter through her high school years. She believes that he can cure all of her ailments and would rather see him than her pediatrician. He has also offered her advice when she has sought it out. He is more than just a doctor. He is a father figure, an uncle, a big brother, and a friend. It's amazing how Doc makes her feel like he is her personal doctor. You could not ask for a better person to have so much influence on your child during the difficult stage of adolescence. I truly have to thank God for having Doc cross our path.

-Denise Shaw
Mother of Keyana Thompson-Shaw,
Long Beach Poly High School Soccer
Long Beach, CA

Dossman Advantage Taping (D.A.T.) is a specialized taping system developed to enhance proprioception, speed, and biomechanics. Doc Dossman has developed multiple applications in both the upper and lower extremities. Here are testimonials from various athletes that have found benefit in this cutting edge system.

Dossman Advantage Tape

"Reflex Running"

www.datdoc.com

**GIMME DAT . . . I NEED DAT
I WANT DAT . . . GOTTA HAVE DAT**

I feel more control . . . I like to maintain a tight rhythm. Doc, I can clearly see where you are going with this. You want to get us all hooked on this so we have to bring you to Europe! I get it. I get it! Because we are gonna be needing this tape job that only you can do! It balances out because we make more money, so you make more money. And then there's more money and more problems for our rivals, who for me, I have quite a few. But if they ain't talking bout you, you ain't doing nothin'! I like that you can feel the difference the tape makes without feeling the tape. It's good to have some help that you can almost forget about!

-Felix Sanchez, Dominican Republic Track & Field
3x World Champion, 400m Hurdles ('01, '03 & '07)
2004 Olympic Gold Medalist, 400m Hurdles

It's helping me out. I haven't had any problems. Everything holds up tight. This is it right here! You wanna try this out! I do like the tape. It feels good! We are going to have to work out a plan for when I leave the country.

-Tasha Danvers, Great Britain Track & Field
2008 Olympic Bronze Medalist, 400m Hurdles

From what I have seen, it seems to help the athletes stay in form. Knee lift and dorsiflexion is enhanced. This makes them more efficient and powerful with less effort. I like that. I see consistencies with all the athletes. I also like how you corrected Tasha Danver's supination.

-Darrell Smith
World-Class Professional Track Coach (DSports)

Testimonials

It feels good! I haven't run track in a few years but I feel like I'm right back on the track! It keeps me aligned and my form right. It also seems to take stress off of my knees and ankles. I really don't feel it [on me] at all. It works on my quickness, cutting, making moves, getting in and out of breaks, and other stuff like that.

-Travon Patterson
USC Trojans Football #17
USC Trojans Track & Field

I just completed a half marathon with the tape. I ran with no pain which is very unusual for me because I have shin splints and all the problems with my legs. My warm-up time is usually about two-to-three miles and I usually don't start to kick until the fourth or fifth mile. With the tape there was no warm-up, I could just go. As I ran and the miles came on, I just seemed to want to sprint faster. If anything, I was exhausted before my legs got tired. I think I was one energy gel short because I know if I had one more packet I could have pushed through hard because the legs were fine! After the race, I am not fatigued. My legs feel fine. I plan on running tomorrow. With the tape I recover so much faster and I don't get the heaviness in my legs. As a matter of fact, I've got a lot of bounce in my legs as I walk even now.

-Danna Duncan
Marathoner

Doc Dossman

It's easier to get my knees up and everything comes more natural. I get a quick reaction and pop, increased turnover, less effort, and my jumps are definitely more explosive. It is easier on my knees . . . I'm 148 pounds feeling like 100!!

-Shana Woods
USC Track & Field, Heptathalon, Long Jump & Relays
High School All-American
Member of National Indoor Record Setting Teams, 800m Relay & 400m Relay, Long Beach Poly
2006 USA Track & Field Jr. Heptathlon Champion
National High School Record Holder in Heptathlon
(First high school girl to ever score over 5,500 points)
2005 U.S. Team for the Youth Championships in Morocco
2004 California State Long Jump Champion

It was so much easier to get off the ground. I don't even practice high jump and I almost [beat my personal record] which is amazing to me. I think it definitely helped my "ups." I'm always feeling on edge. Your muscles feel like they are always ready to go, as if you are in the blocks. I felt like I was running smoother and more in control. I tested it out on hard, solid concrete and still had effortless spring! It felt very responsive and I would not expect that on concrete.

-Rhonda Watkins
UCLA Women's Track & Field, Long Jump/High Jump
2008 Trinidad and Tobago Olympian, Long Jump
2007 NCAA Indoor and Outdoor Champion, Long Jump
2006 World Junior Champion, Long Jump

Testimonials

The push off the ground is a lot easier. I feel like I'm attacking my steps as opposed to trying to lift, recover, and then find the ground. I don't feel the tape. I'm looking at it now, so I know it's there.

-Natasha Hastings, Nike Track & Field
2008 Olympic Gold Medalist (1600m Relay)
2007 NCAA Indoor and Outdoor Champion, 400m
2007 U.S. Outdoor Runner-Up, 400m
2007 SEC Scholar Athlete of the Year
2006 NACAC Silver Medalist, 400m
2005 U.S. Junior Outdoor Champion, 400m
2005 SEC Indoor Runner-Up, 400m
2004 World Junior Champion (400m) and Gold Medalist (1600m Relay)

I like this! It feels really good! I feel a lot of pop and fluent movement. The one thing that I can tell a lot is the pop (from my foot off the ground back up off the ground and back up). It feels really good! I am not a tape person. I don't like to be taped but this isn't uncomfortable. Usually tape is uncomfortable for me and I end up pulling it off but this is pretty good. It doesn't feel like a kinesiotape job (or any other). I also notice that it pushes me so I really have to control the movement. I guess that is from the additional pop that I get from the tape.

-Carmelita Jeter, Fastest Woman Alive
2010 World Indoor Championships Bronze Medalist, 60m
2010 U.S. Indoor Champion, 60m
2009 U.S. Outdoor Champion, 100m
2x World Outdoor Championships Bronze Medalist, 100m

I feel a huge difference running with the tape and without. I would say there's more bounce. My push off seems more powerful. Lately I've been having trouble pushing off on this right leg but I don't feel any pain at all. [Now] it's really easy, so it's definitely doing something! And whatever it's doing, it's good. Running feels effortless for the most part, and it just seemed a lot easier to just pick up my legs and keep going.

-Nicole Leach
UCLA Track & Field Sprinter and Hurdler
4x NCAA All-American ('06, '07, '08, '09)
2009 Pac-10 Champion, 1600m Relay
2007 PanAm Games Bronze Medalist:
400m Hurdles and 1600m Relay
2x NCAA Champion ('07 & '09), 400m Hurdles
2x Pac-10 Champion ('06 & '07), 400m Hurdles
2006 U.S. Junior World Champion, 1600m Relay
3x U.S. Junior National Champion, 400m Hurdles

I think I get more of a comfortable range of motion. I already feel pop without any warm-up. I can definitely feel a balance on both legs. As a hurdler, it's extremely comfortable and my movements are not restricted. With your typical kinesiotape job I feel slightly restricted, but I like that (because it keeps me compact). But for race day you want to be ready to go! Doc Dossman is awesome and I highly recommend him!

-Candice Davis, USA Track & Field
USC Track & Field
2008 World Indoor Championships Silver Medalist, 100m Hurdles

Testimonials

My legs feel good and my feet are aligned in the right direction. I use less energy on the ground. I feel like I'm [being] pushed off the ground. I get more pop/response from the track. My technique on the curve is better. It has helped my achilles pain. I was once afraid to run the curve because of how it made my achilles feel.

-Martial Mbandjock, Mizuno Track & Field
2008 French National Champion, 100m
2009 French National Champion, 200m
2009 World Championships Semi-Finalist 200m
2008 Olympics Semi-Finalist, 100m
2008 World Indoor Championship Semi-Finalist, 100m

The tape helps me with my mechanics. Without the tape everything feels all over the place. When I get up from getting taped, I feel like I'm walking on air. When I get my knee up, it automatically kicks out. It's automatic!

-Turquoise Thompson
UCLA Women's Track & Field Hurdler
2010 Pac-10 Champion, 400m Hurdles
2009 California State Champion, 400m
2009 Nationally Ranked 1st in 400m Hurdles
2008 USA Track & Field National Junior Olympic Young Women's Champion, 400m Hurdles

I get more turnover in my stride, absolute speed, I feel my patella firing, and I gain a noticeable pop.

-Eric Wright
Cleveland Browns NFL Defensive Back, #24

I feel supported. I have been having problems with my knee but now it feels very free. It feels good. I just feel like I can run with this tape on. Some tape jobs make you feel restricted and are tight and you can't move. This allows you to use your form. It felt beautiful and snappy! This is what you need to feel when you are running. That's what I want to feel in a tape job and I found it here.

-Emma Ania, Great Britain Track & Field
2008 Olympian, Women's 400m Relay

I felt bouncier and I got more turnover. I felt quicker. I hit the ground faster. That's how I feel. If I don't feel anything else, I feel lighter and bouncier.

-Joey Hughes
USC Trojans Track & Field Sprinter
2x Pac-10 Champion, 1600m Relay ('09 & '10)
2x Pac-10 Champion, 400m ('09 & '10)
2008 California State Champion, 400m and 1600m Relay

I feel like I'm ready to just go! It's like that tape is lifting my legs. It just feels good. My legs feel good. It's comfortable! It's like I can run easier. Fast breaks . . . I feel like I can go! I felt like I could run up and down the court easier and I could explode out of my moves better. I like it, Doc. I would definitely play with it on.

-April Cook
Washington State Cougars Basketball, #1
2x Pac-10 Conference Honorable Mention
McDonald's All-American Nominee
3x California State Champions (Long Beach Poly)

Testimonials

Before I met this wonderful man of God, I already felt an aura of care, compassion and wisdom . . . I had always heard great things about Doc, but they were minute compared to my experience [with] him . . . In a brief time he led me to believe that anything is possible when you live according to who you are and what you believe in. [He is] a mentor, coach, therapist, father, and a wonderful man of God . . . I always have a notebook handy to make sure I capture the wisdom he has to offer! Children listen because [his] voice resonates [with] where [they] are. Doc [makes] you feel like you are his closest friend. He is one of the few people I [am] able to talk to about anything . . . when I talk to Doc, I always gain knowledge of who I am, where I am going, and the confidence that someone believes [in me] . . . Doc, thank you for being a beacon of light and wisdom in [this] world . . . Thank you for taking the time out to get to know the people [in] your life.

-Todd Covington
Director of Fitness Programming/Exercise Physiologist
Kingley Health
"Transforming Lives"
www.kingleyhealth.com

I notice a faster reaction (to bringing my foot off the ground). It's almost like a rubber band (how it recoils upon stretching). The tape job isn't even noticeable when it is on my body.

-Samie Parker
Oakland Raiders NFL Wide Receiver, #12

Doc Dossman

It helps me with my high knees when I run. I get more bounce and it helps me propel my hips forward. That is always good when you're sprinting. I don't even feel the tape on me. I also like it because it looks cool!

-Akawkaw Ndigpagbor
Long Beach Poly Track & Field
2010 California State Champion, 1600m Relay
2009 California State Champion, 400m Relay
2008 California State Champion, 400m

I normally have to kick my cane out at an angle. I feel better and more balanced. I feel a longer and faster stride. My dorsiflexion is improved so I can stride longer without worrying about hitting my foot. This is very interesting. I like what you are doing. Thank you for doing this for me. I appreciate it!

-Mike Parker, P.T.
Multiple Sclerosis Patient

Affectionately known as "Doc" by all, Dr. Craig Dossman, Jr. is deemed by many as *the* top sports medicine practitioner in Southern California. He is sought out by athletes on every level - pop warner football, youth track, high school, college, and professional - and has become the go to guy for the demographic of youth, ages 12-25.

Words such as passionate, personable, energetic, animated, spiritual, compassionate, no-nonsense, and hilarious are all used to describe this gifted practitioner. Doc is both loved and respected in his beloved Long Beach community for his care and dedication to the youth. Although he is a clinic owner and director who works with the community and various local schools, his reputation was developed through his professional relationship with the Long Beach Polytechnic High School Athletic department, a nationally recognized powerhouse. He is often seen at various sporting events lending his time. Quite simply, he is unorthodox in every way. In fact, you would never know he is a doctor if you met him on the street. You might even mistake him for a patient when you visit his office. Doc is hypomanic, filled with endless energy and ideas, and *always* planning his newest innovation and treatment approach. Compounding his accomplished work in Sports Medicine, he is also the creator of Vocal Biomechanical Rehabilitation (VBR), an unprecedented vocal rehabilitative therapy, the developer/owner of various pending patent ideas such as Dossman Advantage Taping (patent pending), a system that enhances deep tendon reflexes to increase speed and improve muscle recovery in athletes.

Doc Dossman is the owner and clinic director of his sports medicine practice in downtown Long Beach. As if his plate isn't full enough, he serves on the Advisory Board for the Fremont College *Sport Science Program*. He also serves on the *Diversity Council to the President* at the Southern California University of Health Sciences, where he is a *Supervising Doctor for the Post Graduate Internship Program*. A Southern California native, Doc resides in Long Beach with his wife, Rashida and son, Craig III. He enjoys spending time at home with his family, exercising, making people laugh, and is the worship leader at his church.

Looking for a non-profit organization to contribute to? WE GOT NEXT is a non-profit formed to benefit the "next" generation (our kids). This organization provides health education, free sports physicals, and free healthcare to those who do not have health insurance. Tax deductible donations are greatly appreciated and accepted via our website.

Visit www.thehardestpilltoswallow.com
email us at info@thehardestpilltoswallow.com

Visit the author's other websites:
www.docdossman.com
www.youtube.com/lbsportsdoc
www.docdossman.blogspot.com

www.ingramcontent.com/pod-product-compliance
Lightning Source LLC
Chambersburg PA
CBHW070556100426
42744CB00006B/306